CW00384233

*To the memory of
the late Mary MacLean of Ballantrushal
in Lewis.
This was a woman who walked with God
and had deep insight into the world
to come.
She carried many a burden for me
and she was my friend.*

ACKNOWLEDGEMENTS

I am grateful to my wife Isobel and to Miss Pauline Anderson, Mr Alistair Duff and Miss Jennifer Jack for proof-reading and helpful contributions. My daughter Alison processed and helped to edit the material from tape-recordings through various drafts.

REVIVAL
Living in the Realities

Other books by the same author:

REVIVAL

Living in the Realities

Hugh B. Black

NEW DAWN BOOKS
GREENOCK, SCOTLAND

© Hugh B. Black 1993

First published 1993 by
NEW DAWN BOOKS
27 Denholm Street, Greenock PA16 8RH, Scotland

All rights reserved.
No part of this publication may be reproduced,
stored in a retrieval system, or transmitted,
in any form or by any means, electronic, mechanical,
photocopying, recording or otherwise without the
prior permission in writing from the publishers.

ISBN 1 870944 17 8

Unless otherwise stated, biblical references
are to the Revised Version.

Production and Printing in England for
NEW DAWN BOOKS
27 Denholm Street, Greenock PA16 8RH, Scotland by
Nuprint Ltd, Station Road, Harpenden, Herts AL5 4SE.

Contents

Christ's Response — What of You? — A Hard Saying —
Invitation

FOREWORD

I have known Mr Black since secondary school, when he was my history teacher, and through his preaching I found Christ as Saviour. Since then, over the last twenty-seven years, I have had the privilege of being taught in the things of God through his preaching and ministry.

It has been my joy over these years to see increasing numbers of people find physical healings, deliverance and needs of every kind met by God through his ministry.

I have found the author has been a tremendous encouragement to me to believe God for great things, and I pray that this book will inspire you to go forward in God and to expect His burning, reviving fire to be poured out over our land.

Joan Jewell

EXPLANATORY NOTE

In this book there is an attempt to take readers in spirit into the meetings in which the teaching now produced in written form was first presented. This accounts for the inclusion of prayers, exhortations, and other linking material. (Initials enclosed in square brackets after the heading of such items denote the individual, other than the author, through whom some of this material came). Obviously a listening audience was first addressed — but now the material is adapted to suit a reading audience also.

A similar approach has been taken in my most recent books, including *Christian Fundamentals*, *Pioneers of the Spiritual Way*, and the first two volumes of the *Revival* trilogy. These seem to have been happily received; I trust that this too will be generally approved.

INTRODUCTION

This book is the third of a trilogy. The first, *Revival: Including the Prophetic Vision of Jean Darnall*, majored on revivals long past. The second, *Revival: Personal Encounters*, featured movements of God nearer our own time. The present volume envisages Christian life and activity in the wake of revival.

Revival will not perfect the church. Instruction will still be required. Revival will, however, have taken certain barriers out of the way and the church will be in a position to attain high heights with God.

The sermons on which this book is based were preached after a series on revival and envisaged Christians in a revived condition meeting the challenge and demands of life on a higher plane. The realities of this dimension and what is entailed in living in it are reflected in the chapter headings, for example, 'Imitators of Christ', 'Beyond Forgiveness to Love', 'Beyond Acceptance to Rejoicing', 'Spiritual Warfare'.

We should always remember that although we may experience revival all is not accomplished in our spiritual lives as a result. We should expect to have high aspirations for God, and in the new environment have faith to reach ever upward; we should have achievable goals, and experience ever deepening sanctification. Many Christians are familiar with the basic teaching of death to self and know at least intellectually if not experimentally how this works — but there can come the realization that there are varying depths of this. This book does not attempt merely to go over old fundamental teaching on Christian behaviour, but rather indicates some of the highest standards asked by God. For example, forgiveness of our enemies is not enough: we are asked to love them not only for Christ's sake and theirs but for our own. Acceptance of our cross must be surpassed by our rejoicing in it.

Spiritual warfare will continue, and there is an attempt to deal with some of the practical issues involved. Testimonies from people who have experience of this realm are included.

Finally, in a world where revival has been experienced and is continuing, healing may well be a prominent feature of church life. A chapter of this book is devoted to a 'cluster' of recent healings. What is particularly noteworthy about the account of these is the sense of the living Christ present in each one and dominating the awareness of those whose bodies were healed.

Revival, after all, involves the awareness of the Christ and living in the reality of His presence in the world.

1 | **I HAVE A DESTINY**

EXHORTATION AND PRAYER [MB]: *Oh, catch the sense of the power of the living Christ, the risen and ascended Christ. Catch a sense of the truth that the Christ whom we worship is on the throne of glory, and there is no power, no weapon forged against Him that shall prosper. He alone is the Son of God, He alone has that place before God, in God. There is no other name on earth or in Heaven by which man shall be saved. There is one way to the Father, Christ risen, glorified.*

O God, we feel the wave of that love beating at the door of our heart, seeking an entry that we might become a channel of that love to the lost souls of humanity, that we shall not only receive your love, but, O Lord, we shall be channels of that love. We pray for an increased measure of that love to find access into us and through us. As we sense the power of the ocean beat, we know that we are carrying a thimbleful of that love, when we could become as open doors through which the waves of the ocean cascade forth. O Father, teach us Your way, that a path shall be made for this people, to the glory of God. Of You, O Lord, we ask these things. Amen.

> PROPHECY: *Steep steps lead upward, a*
> *narrow path beckons, a ribbon of light*
> *stretches on ahead. Take the ribbon of*
> *light at decision point. Take the road*
> *that seems narrow, that ever leads*
> *upward. Be not afraid: I guarantee My*
> *peace.*

Three Trees and Their Destiny

Recently I came across a reading which is very relevant
to our present study. It described three trees, each of
which had a destiny.

Three large trees in a forest prayed that they might choose
what they would be converted into when they were felled.
One prayed to be made into a beautiful palace; the second,
to be a large ship to sail the seven seas; the third, to stay in
the forest and always point toward God.

One day the woodman came and chopped down the
first tree, but instead of a palace, it was made into a
common stable, wherein was born the fairest Babe in all
creation. The second tree was made into a small ship that
was launched on the Sea of Galilee, on the deck of which
stood a tall young man who told the multitudes: 'I am
come that they might have life, and that they might have it
more abundantly.' The third tree was made into a cross,
and to it men nailed that young man, the loveliest person-
ality that ever walked the earth. Ever since then, that cross
has been pointing men to God. And so each prayer was
answered.[1]

Our Individual Roles

'I have a destiny': so runs the chorus that we sometimes
sing.

In pondering the theme of individual destiny, I have

realized that again and again God comes on me in a way that makes preaching very personal, very practical, and very much related to those of you who hear it. It is not vague and general, not airy-fairy, far-away and nebulous, but immediately applicable. Indeed, to produce action I repeatedly use the same illustration, about a table spread and the frustration of being unable to eat the food.

Picture the scene. The public hall is booked until 10 p.m. The people sit down at the loaded tables at 8 p.m. The chairman introduces various people to speak of food and nutrition. A farmer tells of its production, a baker of its processing, a nutritionist of its food value, a dietician of its use and abuse. It is a most informative evening. Food has been discussed up hill and down dale. Many obtain a greater understanding from the various lectures. Suddenly at 9:45 p.m. the chairman glances at his watch and in a startled voice indicates that we must all go home — with the rich banquet untouched. We have run out of time and the caretaker is very particular about these things. Imagine your reaction. Yet so often in the spiritual world does this not happen? There is a danger that a sermon may be preached and people think, 'Yes, that's right, that's good,' and so on, and go home to bed without taking any action on what is taught. For a long time now I have felt that when you spread the table and show the people the provision, you should not suggest that they go home; rather you invite them to come to the table and eat, and to do it right there and then. It is like that with this preaching. It is for action now, for response now.

Great Men of Other Days

But there is a difficulty here. I realize that as I preach about the possibilities that are in life for people, I frequently take cases from the Bible or from recent history. And I think that many of you can be almost totally cut off from what I am saying. For example, I can speak of the action of God in the lives of Abraham, Noah, Moses, Jacob, Joshua, Shadrach, Meshach, Abednego, Daniel, and the rest of the Old Testament's prophets and saints. I can come to the New Testament and speak of Paul, Peter, John, Barnabas, and great men of that day. I can jump to more modern times and speak of Finney, Wesley, Spurgeon, Hudson Taylor, C.T. Studd, Rees Howells and other names with which you are now very familiar. It has rather escaped me that you may hear me and be saying, 'Yes, I believe that God worked mightily in the lives of these men. I believe that they were men of destiny, men called of God, and they were born for their age and for the divine purpose. Paul was a chosen vessel. But I'm only Jimmy Jones, I'm only Jean Hendry from round the corner. I'm no Paul, I'm no Abraham, I'm no Moses, I'm no Jacob: I'm just me.' (As the children's chorus has it: 'I just thank You, Father, for making me me' — I have always had a question-mark as I look around you and wonder why you are all so thankful!)

But you are you. And you see these mighty men and women of old, and you feel, 'What you say is true: it's true for them. But what about me? I'm just a very ordinary person, I'm just me, and what have you to say to me?'

I've got this to say to you. If you are a son or a daughter of Adam's race, there is for you a destiny, there is a calling, there is a role that no-one else in all the world, in all of time or eternity will ever fulfil.

There is a role for you, there is a place for you — and a higher place than God's place for you, you cannot have. It is perfectly fitted for you, and it suits you altogether.

Occasionally I tell you of an early Pentecostalist who in a vision of Heaven saw the crown room, and there was one crown above all others that caught his attention and dazzled him with its extreme beauty. His guide spoke to him and said,

'Which of the crowns do you like best?'

There was no question. One crown outshone all others, and he chose it. The guide said,

'Everybody feels the same about the crown that is prepared for him.'

He then showed him the cross room. And there was one cross that was hideous. It was absolutely awful in his view. It was twisted, dark, knotted. Of all the crosses on display that was by far the worst. The guide said,

'Everybody thinks that about the cross that is for him.'

I can imagine that as he was lifted on to that cross, everywhere it touched, it hurt: there were in the wood knots that hurt every vulnerable part of his body. And he was told, 'If you want to wear the crown, you must bear the cross.'

As the cross and the crown are both perfectly fitted for you, so is your individual role in life. It is peculiarly yours. You 'have a destiny' and it is yours and no other's.

Greener Grass in Distant Fields

I know so many of you so well, and you talk to me. Many of you think that if you were asked to carry someone else's burden it would be quite easy; you could stand it; but the burden that is on you is almost unbearable. You look at another person's life, and you think, 'Oh, if only I had that calling it would be wonderful.' You covet that calling. You think that your cross is the worst. Now because I happen to know many of your particular cases, I could often say to a person, 'Look, I know your circumstances are horrendous. But there are half-a-dozen people present, known to both of us, who are in a far, far worse position than you are right now.' Of course I don't do that, because it's not for me to convey information about any one of you to any other. But take my word for it that there are many who think their case is worst of all, when it is nothing of the kind.

An animal often thinks that the grass in another field is greener than that on which it grazes — that the far-away grass is more luscious than the grass at its feet. You will see a horse stretch its neck over a barbed-wire fence to get at the grass on the other side. There is plenty of food at its feet, but it risks getting its throat cut to get at the food that's somewhere else. And people are like that. They think they would be happier somewhere else. If only they could change their circumstances, how happy they could be; but in the circumstances in which they are, how impossible life is. There is a thorn in the flesh — 'Oh, God, I could stand anything but this thorn, and I've asked You again and again to take it away, and You leave it there.' Unlike many of us, Paul was very sharp spiritually. He ultimately realized that his particular thorn was pressing him into Christ, he was getting into a deeper life with Christ, and he was knowing Christ more intimately — and so he blessed the thorn that drove him there, and he rejoiced in his weakness, because in weakness the strength of God was revealed.

So now I am tying you into your own situation as it is at present, not as you would like it to be — very much in line with the sentiments in that hymn that is so often sung as people come to Christ:

> Just as I am, without one plea,
>   But that Thy blood was shed for me,
> And that Thou bid'st me come to Thee,
>   O Lamb of God, I come.
>
> Just as I am, and waiting not
>   To rid my soul of one dark blot,
> To Thee, whose blood can cleanse each spot,
>   O Lamb of God, I come.

Just as I am. And these are my words to you: just as you are, and just where you are, is exactly where God is prepared to meet you, to rescue you, to change you, to make your life into a thing of glory.

The Uniqueness of Your Call

Just think of it. You have a destiny and a role to fulfil that no-one else in all the world has. And if you don't do it, and it is not fulfilled in you, it will never happen in all the universe. You are born to show forth a particular light and radiance of Christ that none other will ever show.

You can picture a jeweller's window, the diamonds flashing in the sun. They are all reflecting the same sun, but they are all giving off a different glory according to how they have been cut. You are 'cut' by God in a particular way, and no other in all the world is 'cut' in precisely that way; no two blades of grass are the same; no two people are the same. There is a glory that God wants reflected from your life that will never come from another life in all of time or eternity. And for that, my friend, you will give an account to God. If you come short in your reflection of Christ, you will answer before the throne of God.

And Death to Self

You say, 'What does God want me to do?'

You will be shocked at the answer: 'Nothing. Nothing. Nothing.'

'Oh,' you say, 'that's easy. I've been doing nothing for a long time. I'm good at it.' Some of you may indeed say that very truthfully! But it is not that kind of 'nothing' I am talking about. Quite frequently as the soul begins to pursue its goal, you want to work for God, you want to witness for Christ, you want to preach the gospel, or you want to teach Scripture. This is all very understandable. Perchance you want to receive gifts of the Spirit, you want to be used in the church in utterances in tongues bearing interpretation; you want to be used in interpretation, prophecy, discernment, miracles, faith, wisdom, knowledge, and so on. It may be you particularly want the gifts of healing, that you may be seen of men.

You move out in all of these directions to do something, *to do something*. And when the motives are good, God appreciates it (if I might use such a phrase in connection with God). I believe that He sees the desire of every honest heart, that He understands every aspiration that rises in every child of His. He understands it all. But, you know, He has something far deeper for us than what we normally conceive. You would like to take your portion. You would like to have your birthright now. You want to go out and work for God. You would like to have healing under your hand, so that you could heal; you would like to be able to do this, and be able to do that. Do you know, you will never have that; He will not do that with you. That is not what He wants. The word gift is not in the original.[2] What are described as gifts in 1 Corinthians 12 are operations of the Spirit that come through human channels. They are not envisaged as being under human control for you to manipulate and use. Rather you are seen as being used in them. Learn that God is to be in control, and that you can do nothing.

> My hands were filled with many things
>> That I did precious hold
> As any treasure of a king,
>> Silver, gems, or gold.
> The Master came and touched my hands;
>> 'I must have empty hands', said He,
>> 'Wherewith to work My works through thee.'

God doesn't want you to do anything.

So you say, 'What does God want with me? What does God want?'

God wants your funeral. You will say, 'This is a hearty preacher we've got.' God wants your funeral pyre. He wants to see an end of you. He wants to see you buried in that box ten fathoms deep, never to appear any more.

'What, all my loveliness? all my good looks? all my attractive qualities? all my natural abilities, my eloquence, my understanding, my brains?'

The lot. He doesn't want a picking of them — not a picking of them. You see, He wants them crucified and He works a transformation. The old man dies and the new man lives. Old carnal gifts and qualities are changed and Christ shines through them.

An Interesting Interlude

This takes me back in memory. I had been invited to speak to an interdenominational meeting many years ago. One or two of our congregation went there fairly regularly. These were very amiable people, and they were trusted to behave peaceably and not rock too many boats. What the leaders of the meeting did not realize was that their friends were leading a 'wolf' into their midst in the shape of me. I had a message to deliver, and I didn't particularly look to see what the interdenominational title was above the door: God had given me a message, and that was all there was about it.

I remember the meeting started with some fairly modern guitar music; the person concerned was lauded as a wonderful gift to the church, and I was feeling worse and worse. The time came for me to speak. The hand of the Lord was upon me, and I took the rubbish of human gift and human attainment, and told that company that God wanted these things buried, our every natural talent and gift buried.

I remember the end of the meeting. It wasn't convenient to 'tarry' there, but I took one young man out to my car, where he had a wonderful baptism in the Spirit. Ultimately I left him staggering on the pavement, hardly able to stand, from where he went to another gathering and created consternation there by telling the wonderful thing that had happened to him. These memories all come back now. God wanted that musician's gift crucified, the ego crucified, human adulation crucified. And, my friend, He wants that in your life and in mine.

Christ in You

You say, 'He doesn't want me to work for Him, and now you tell me He doesn't really want me to go on living, He wants me dead — tell me, what does God want?'

Paul said, *O wretched man that I am! who shall deliver me from this body of death?* (Rom 7:24). *I have been crucified with Christ; yet I live; and yet no longer I, but Christ liveth in me* (Gal 2:20). The *old* Paul nailed to that cross. The resurrected Jesus living in the body of the *new* Paul. Not I, but Christ. I can imagine some of you saying in your heart, 'Poetic, airy-fairy language, a multiplicity of words, a nice word-picture.' My friend, let me tell you: I am down to earth. I have kept my feet on the ground for more years than I'm going to confess to.

I remember noticing the outworking of this principle with Miss Taylor.[3] One day someone phoned her in deep need, and she ministered to them on the phone. Later in speaking to me she said, 'You know, I don't know what I was doing there. I didn't do anything. Something happened, but I had nothing to do with it.' I remember saying to her, 'That is why you were there: because you have the ability to get out of the way and let the life of Christ pass through. That is precisely why.'

Similarly you may pick up an old letter of Miss Taylor's, and after reading the first two lines you may suddenly find that the Spirit has fallen: she had gone into the Spirit and wasn't writing as Miss Taylor; she was a channel of the living God. That is one reason why her letters were so effective to so many people.

Now let me bring things down to very clear-cut terms. What generally happens is this. To people coming for ministry, if they have been baptized in the

Spirit, I say, 'Go into the Spirit.' I deliberately wait for the action of God to affect them — and something of God passes through. At that point they may be healed.

You may not happen to feel like ministering. Recently in the vestry there was a powerful, awful deliverance. I was physically very tired at the time; but that was irrelevant. You put all the human part of you aside and you become conscious of the anointing of the holy. God wants nothing but an open channel, totally at his disposal. That is one of the high points of our spiritual life. It is not the only high point. There is another side to things — that as the old man decays and dies the new man lives and develops. You grow into the maturity of a full-grown man or woman in Christ. Christ grows within you, and He is manifested through you; He emanates from you, and people meet Christ in you. They are not blessed through *you*, you understand, but through the Christ who lives in you.

A Road of Real Power

That's too humble a road, perchance, for people who want a name. People who want human adulation may find this teaching distasteful. But, I tell you, this is a victory that overcomes the world. It is a victory that overcomes the power of Satan. Satan can put up with you endlessly — he's not afraid of you or of me. But he cannot stand the Son of God. In the moment Jesus comes into one of these occasions of deliverance Satan flees, absolutely flees the field. He is terrified of the lowly, humble Son of God. Satan with all his power quails before that name. Not, of course, before the vain repetition of the name (you can be as foolish about that as about other things, e.g. the idea of cleansing through a vain 'applying of the blood'); it is not merely the use of such a phrase or the repetition of the name that brings effective action. It is the moving of the power of God.

I remember being terribly strongly opposed once in a deliverance situation. During the course of ministry I instructed someone to envisage at its worst the thing that had caused a demon to enter. The person interrupted to say that as they did this the situation was getting worse: they were going into the sin, and indeed wanted the sin. The soul lusted after the filth of it. I said in my heart, 'O God, what can I do? I can't be responsible for taking this person into deepening mire' — nor could I easily retreat, because I instinctively resist the idea of quitting the field and leaving victory with Satan. But, you know, in a glorious moment Christ came. He had been with me before, but He came then in a particular way. I can't explain that; I just felt it. *He* came. And I remember saying, 'Glory be to God,' or words to that effect. (Now I am not a very expressive person; my hallelujahs tend to be confined to that point where demons are going out, when outside observers might be scared stiff — then the glory of God is in my soul, because I know that to be the hour of victory.) Suddenly in that case I knew the hour had come and I said, 'I have nothing more to do with this matter. Christ is here.' That demon didn't stay to argue longer. No talk of plunging into filth any more — oh, no, Christ was there. It is the action of Christ that counts. That action of Christ effects immediate miracle. It flashes under our eyes as we minister. It can flash across hundreds of miles of telephone wire as the sick are prayed for, as haunted houses are cleansed. Wonderful is the action of Christ in a moment of time.

Empty but Full

'So', you say, 'am I just going to be an empty channel, of
no more value than the dish that holds the flowers?'
No, He fills you with Himself. You are not an empty
vessel. You are a vessel who is emptied and then filled
with God. You have intimate contact with Christ. You
live in Him, you live in the Spirit, you live in Christ
and Christ lives in you.

You can be (if I may say this reverently, and I am
careful of my wording) a Christ person, and Christ can
live His life through you. You can become like Christ in
your day and generation, no matter who you are. You
can start right now to put on Christ, yes, to *put on
Christ.* He will become a miracle-worker through you,
and you may develop into the fullness of a full-grown
man or woman in Christ. Can you imagine a higher
destiny?

Christ Pre-eminent

I have sometimes pictured the great men and women of
all the ages gathered. Imagine a vast hall, and the
Napoleons and the Caesars and the generals and the
statesmen and the kings from all the ages, the greatest
potentates of all time are together there. You are given
an offer: which of these would you most like to re-
semble? Stay a moment. There is one more to arrive.
And the Lord Jesus comes into the midst of that company. Surely no eye would then be fixed on Churchill
or Napoleon. Every eye would turn to Christ, the Lord
of lords and the King of kings. Do you realize that God's
offer to you is that you can be like Jesus? Not Napoleon,
not Churchill, none of the second-raters (compared to
Christ), but Christ Himself. Realize what your potential
is. Believe in your destiny, embrace your calling,

understand the possibilities that God holds out to every soul. You can start from where you are, and you can start right now. Blessed be His name.

Invitation

I ask those of you to whom God has been speaking to respond — those of you who really feel that there is hope, that you could start now to put on the Lord Jesus and become a different person. You remember it was said of Saul that when the Spirit of the Lord came on him he became a different person. You too can become a different person. Bring yourself to a point of commitment. Do business with God. Of the broken clay He makes another vessel. He is able to change you, to take the broken thing and to make it whole again. If you have failed on the first plan that God had for your life, He will give you another plan.

He is like a master painter. If someone slung an ink-bottle at a white wall of your home, leaving a hideous stain, a real artist could so paint round it that it could become a thing of beauty. If you had the services of a Michelangelo or a Raphael, you could have a painting made with that horrible thing at the very centre of it, transformed into a thing of beauty for ever, eagerly sought by people from all over the world.

And so Christ can take your life with all the smudge and the stain, and He can create something new. He will not paint round the stain; He will cover it over with His own blood, and He will give you a clean, fresh start. Blessed be the name of God.

Notes

1 Mrs Charles Cowman, *Streams in the Desert* vol. 2 (Marshall Pickering, 1966; © 1966 Cowman Publications, Inc.), reading for 23 April.
2 See Hugh Black, *Reflections on the Gifts of the Spirit* (New Dawn Books, 1988), chap. 1.
3 Founder member and co-leader of the Struthers fellowship. Her story is told in the author's *A Trumpet Call to Women* (New Dawn Books, 1988), part 2. Further information is given in the author's *Gospel Vignettes* (New Dawn Books, 1989), Appendix: 'The Ministry of the Revelation of Christ'.

2 | IMITATORS OF CHRIST

PRAYER: *Lord our God, we pray for the sense of the anointing of the Holy Spirit. O God, there is joy in our hearts. We rejoice at Your action. We rejoice in the healing of bodies; we rejoice in the baptism in the Holy Spirit; we rejoice in the salvation of souls. We thank You that You have been doing all of these things. We praise Your name. But, O God, we realize that there are other works that You would do in the hearts of men. There are matters, it may be, that are more strongly contested by the wicked one than any of these things that we have mentioned, and O God, we pray that we shall come into alignment with Thy will, have an understanding of Thy will and move, O God, along the lines of Thy choosing. We ask it in the name Lord Jesus Christ and for His sake. Amen.*

When there is a time of rejoicing in Spirit in the work of God, and a feeling of great freedom, it is often a time to be very careful in case we miss anything of what God has for us. I would like to be careful now that we get just exactly what God may have prescribed for us on this present occasion.

A Prophetic Vision

There came to my knowledge a prophecy that Miss Mary Black gave very recently. It was very pointed and quite dramatic, presenting one of those pictures that tend to remain in the memory. The picture is of a ship sailing towards the horizon, over which are dawning the first beams of light from the rising sun. The ship had no compass, no planned course of its own, but steered straight into that beam of light. Light speaks of Christ Himself; the destination is Christ, or Heaven. Part way along that journey, as the voyager turned around, there was an awareness that right in the wake of that ship there were many other smaller ships which could not at first see the light for themselves, but were following after the one that had caught the vision. Because that one knew the way, they were able to follow with confidence.

I think you can understand that very readily. I am sure that all over the world there have been many, many people who had a very dim idea of God and Heaven, till one day the words of an evangelist like Billy Graham came by the power of the Spirit into their beings, and they found Christ. But there were many things about Christ they did not know, and many things about the new life they did not know, and they very naturally began to look to others to show them the way. Now I know there can be dangers in following man — but not if the individual is a true follower of Christ and is living properly.

The verse that I have particularly in mind is this:

Be ye imitators of me, even as I also am of Christ (1 Cor 11:1)

Before the end of the study I may be saying to my

listening audience, 'Would those of you who could say this without a blush or a lie stand to your feet?' I don't reckon that a great number will be standing. I will certainly not be standing. I'll sit down at that point. But I will be interested to see if any of the rest of you can say what Paul said: *Be ye imitators of me, even as I also am of Christ.* I will leave my reading audience to make their own assessments.

Ships at Sea

I pondered the prophecy. I pondered the sailing on the sea first of all. Our every life is like a ship at sea, and while the sea can be very interesting and very attractive, it can also be very dangerous. On a calm night you may look across the waters, and they are quiet and restful and beautiful in the sunset. But there are other times when it is not like that. The waters may grow tempestuous. Have you ever been in a motor boat, or a vessel of that kind, when the storm suddenly broke? I remember travelling in a little craft when the engine stopped, and I can tell you that a motor boat without an engine in a tempestuous sea is a dangerous place to be.

The sea has perils. There are hidden rocks and reefs. There are sudden storms and mighty winds that can quickly rise. You can be in great danger on the ocean, particularly if you are not skilled in sea craft. And in the ocean of life there are many hidden dangers, in your spiritual life hidden reefs, sudden squalls, troubles rising on every hand, skies growing dark. You can be lost, never a star shining, compass broken, going round in circles, making shipwreck. All of these conditions can touch us.

I remember a friend teaching me how to steer a motor boat. You may think, 'Surely that's just automatic. Any-

one could steer a motor boat, just like steering a car.'
But it is not just like steering a car, because in a car you
are on a hard, stable road. In a boat you are on water
that pitches and tosses, rises and falls. You may get
your eye on your destination on the opposite shore and
think that will do. But this is not enough. What you
need to do is to get a fixed point on the boat, say, at the
bow, as well as the point you are aiming to reach on
land. You must line up these two points, and as you
keep them in line you will steer a straight course.

And in the spiritual sense, mark the prophecy. There
was a shining pathway over the waters, leading right
into the presence of God. Now His Word is a light that
shines on our path, and I maintain that any man or
woman who wants to walk in the light *can* walk in the
light. Note that there are two fixed points — the Word
and Heaven. And here in the vision is a craft: here is
one who is moving straight into the glory of God, going
straight to Christ. Such a one can say, *Be ye imitators of
me, even as I also am of Christ.*

A Time for Introspection

Next I began to ponder our individual lives, my own
life, your lives, things I know about you, things that
you bring to me, things that I know about myself. I
thought, 'Yes, that's not like Christ…and that's not like
Christ.' Things rise, and they're not like Christ — and
you can all ponder for yourselves. From your wakening
in the morning, consider what you do, the moods you
display, how you treat others in the family, how you
react to them if you happen to be a slow wakener and
they happen to be like the birds that rise in the morning — full of life at the first dawn of day. They can be a
tribulation to somebody who doesn't want to talk at all

at that particular point. And the person who doesn't want to talk at all can be a bit of a headache to the person who does. Many a needless row has started at the breakfast table because of this.

Take a close look at yourself. Never mind the sins of your friends; just take a walk with yourself. Picture yourself as you go into work, how you react, how certain things annoy you, how you treat other people, and how you resent their treatment of you. You can go through your own day at your leisure; you can go through your own week; you can go through your own month. As I pondered, I thought, 'There's no future in this.' I could talk to you all night about the sins of humanity — and I don't really need to, because you can fill in a list of the sins of humanity without any help from me. If you have any difficulty, just think about somebody who annoys you, and you'll get a list right away! And remember, in the illustration used by the Rwanda missionaries of whom I have often spoken, when you are pointing a finger at someone, another three fingers are pointing back at you. There are certain small defects, perhaps, in you that you hadn't noticed — but others have noticed them, all right. I could see no future in merely listing human failure, because sin proliferates. Un-Christlike conduct is endemic: a chronic condition.

Thorns and Thistles

I was reminded of a country scene. There came a time in the year to cut down thistles and nettles, and you knew as you were cutting that you were merely preventing them spreading. You were not killing them. In these days we did not have chemicals to do that. We knew that the weeds would be up next year in exactly the same places. Then there were the dockens. These multiply very quickly and strongly, and if you merely cut them down you make no progress. We used to try to get the docken out by the root — which is very difficult if it's a big plant. The roots go deep. And you have to get the whole of the root out, or the docken is going to sprout in the next year.

When I look across a congregation, or look into my own heart, I become aware that there is little point in just cutting off wrong things at the surface. For example, it is not enough to say, when you have a bad reaction, 'I'll need to watch that. The next time I'm angry I'll bottle it up and I'll not show it.' You will still emanate it, although you don't realize this, and others will pick it up. You know the situations that arise:

'You were really angry!'

'I didn't say a word!' Righteous indignation. 'Why do you think I was angry?'

'It's perfectly obvious you were angry.'

And indeed it was. Don't let's deceive ourselves. That is how we live. God has some better thing for us. But while these things are all there, we dare not say to anyone, 'Be an imitator of me, as I also am of Christ,' because we realize we are not showing forth Christ steadily in all aspects of our living. We are showing forth Christ selectively. The parts of Christianity that suit, we are radiating. And the parts of Christianity that we haven't come to terms with, we are effectively denying. We are really allowing the 'old man' to go on developing, and we are not in these areas reflecting Christ.

Reflecting Christ

I want to give you a moment's pause to think. In every aspect of your life, are you reflecting the Lord Jesus Christ? What areas of your life are not reflecting Him? What do you propose to do about these areas? I have a great objection to preaching being something up in the sky — high and dry. For me again and again the purpose of preaching is to bring change, immediate change. And as I pondered this, I had no liberty merely to go in detail into the individual sins that appear on the surface of life. What God wants is change at the foundation of life. He wants to change us, to have sin out by the root as He effects these changes: in short, to make each of us a different person. As I meditated, it struck me that Christians can be divided into two categories. The vast majority of us may be grouped in category A, manifesting many un-Christlike traits. In category B, the numbers are not so great. When you view these lives you sense a fragrance and a savour of Christ. Instinctively you feel, 'If I lost my way I could follow that man, that woman, into Heaven. I could trust that person. There is a something there that gives me confidence. I find Christ there.'

Heroes of Old

A number of them came to my mind, names that you often hear. I thought of Hudson Taylor, and I saw a man who had his eyes set on the Glory Land. He had a fixed point as he moved onwards: it was the cross of Jesus Christ. And he steered a remarkably straight course. Occasionally he may have taken a wrong step, made a wrong choice that he quickly regretted and put right. If for a moment he went out of the will of God, one thing I believe he always did immediately was get back into the right place. A life may be committed, and it may stumble; Satan may overtake it over this or that. But the man who is sold out to God quickly comes back into line and keeps that true course.

I thought of George Müller, living so close to God, feeding a vast multitude of children in the Bristol orphanage, walking with God — a man who was sold out to God. I felt I could follow and trust such a man. He has not an axe to grind; he is not pushing a pet theory. His concentration is on God. He wants God Himself. He is not peddling a party line; he is not following a denominational goal. He is following the Lord Jesus. Yes, I could trust such a man.

I thought of Rees Howells. He was a man who had a very single eye for the glory of God and a very single mind, a man of great integrity. Praying Hyde was in the same category. C.T. Studd likewise was a man sold out for God. 'If Jesus Christ be God and died for me, then no sacrifice can be too great that I can make for Him.' In Charles Finney we see another whose goal was God Himself. He turned much of a world upside down, and in a sense goes on turning it upside down, and will do so until the Lord comes, because of the effect of his teaching. Such men were princes with God, committed men, sold-out men. As I pondered, it became very clear to me that God wants total commitment. When a man or a woman is totally committed, there is an emanation of Christ. They do not have to worry about all the details of life then. They do not have to be too concerned about the periphery of life, because they are now going to react spontaneously the way Christ reacted. You see, Christ is going to grow in them and develop in them, and the reaction of Jesus Christ is going to become their spontaneous reaction in every circumstance of life.

A Blessed Hope

You may wonder at my teaching thus. It is in fact a compliment. Let me tell you what I mean by that. Of my listening audience, I believe that there are an increasing number who are prepared for this challenge, who are deeply desirous of this way of life. More in our midst are prepared to pay the price for this than there have ever been from our beginnings, many more. I know many of you so well, I know your integrity, I know your desire, your purpose; and I believe that you can now receive this teaching. I want each of you to realize this: from the moment you are committed to this kind of living, from the point of view of the world you are going to seem a hopeless fanatic. You are going to be one whose priority every day in life is what God wants, not what suits you or what is comfortable. The question is not, 'Where do I want to go? what do I want to do?' but, 'Where does God want me to go? what does God want me to do?' From being a person with your own life, on to which is built something for God, you become a person with God's life, and on to that life there are attachments that God allows. He is central; you are not central. No other person in the world is central. Christ is central, and He dictates the going, and He dictates the speed of the going.

It comes down to very practical issues. It comes down to things like spending a week in the presence of God at one of our forthcoming camps. It can come down to a choice between that and a purely recreational activity. Now, mark, there are times when Christ will lead you into recreational activities. Christ is no killjoy. Let me say that clearly.

I remember a time in earlier days when a wise woman of God insisted that I go to America for two weeks, both for my daughter Alison's sake and for my own. She sensed that I was deeply fatigued and in need of going away. That can happen to a person. God will take care of all your needs. But your life will be dominated by the will of God. You will dwell in God. If you are absorbed in a work of God and someone says, 'Would you not like to have a weekend in Paris?' wild horses would not get you to Paris — you are so taken up with what God is doing. A love draws you on for the thing God wants. You really do become absorbed in the work of God.

If the anointing of God is on me to write, I write through much of the night with great joy. I do not feel a martyr because I am working for hours during the night. It is a glorious privilege to be alone with God and sense the anointing of the Spirit, sense the revelation of God and sense the choice of His words, to be with God in the silence. You are absorbed, you are involved in the thing that God is doing. Your whole life changes by the degree to which you come into this way of life.

Now I don't want to give you any wrong impressions. I am not going to stand and tell you to be an imitator of me. There are other matters that I would not be asking you to imitate.

Time for Commitment

Shall we get down to hard action? I want you to make a conscious commitment to be sundered unto God for His purposes — to become like Paul. What a man, driving on and on and on after they tried to stone him and kill him! Did it change him? Not for a moment — unless it stiffened him in his resolve to go all the way with God. *I press on…I count not myself yet to have apprehended.* One thing he did: he pressed on, to *the prize of the high calling of God*. These are lovely words: the prize of the high calling of God. Do you want the high calling of God? Do you want the prize of the high calling? Or are you content to paddle along in the shallows, a little bit for God and a big bit for self, hoping to make the eternal shore? Or have you the iron? If you haven't, God can give you it, whereby you say, 'Lord, I have only one life; it will soon be past. I'll have only one day of opportunity; it will soon be gone. I devote myself entirely to Your service and Your purposes and Your Person for time and eternity, without the possibility of ever reversing my choice. I want the shoreline cut. I want to be sundered unto God.' Then when you reach the celestial shore and you turn again, you may well have the privilege of seeing countless others following who never themselves had such a clear view of that shore but who are coming on behind because you showed them the way. You yourself held to the course and refused to move off the path of light. You refused to turn to the right or the left, and if temporarily disturbed, tormented and diverted, you came immediately back to the centre of the shining way. No side tracks there on your own, no neglecting of sanctification for convenient occasions. You were gripped of God, controlled of God.

As Paul reviewed his life, he said, *Be ye imitators of me.* He might have said, 'I know many of you as yet cannot see what I see. But *be imitators of me as I am of Christ.*

I can see Christ in my mind's eye, in my spiritual vision; I can see Him. In so far as I can honestly do it, I would like to say, 'Be imitators of me, as I am of Him.' I would love to think that before the end of your days there are many of you who will be able to say in truth to your people in your various groupings, 'If you are not seeing the way too clearly, imitate me. I see it, and I'll lead you to the high heights of God. After you have been following a little way, you will not need me. You will become a ship on your own, on that shining highway.' We don't train people to lean on leaders; we train people ultimately to lean on Christ alone.

Invitation

I am asking those of you to whom the Holy Spirit has been speaking, or those of you who feel that there is something real here for you, to make that total commitment. Come to the place where you are reflecting nothing but Christ. Come though the way may be stormy, though the waves are rising and falling, though Paul is in prison and stoned and left for dead. Even when the waves ride high he never loses that shining pathway. Would those of you to whom God may be speaking, who feel a real desire to come into a way of commitment deeper than you have ever known, take the decisive step?

3 | LOVE ABOVE ALL THOUGHT AND WONDER

PRAYER [MB]: *O God, we sense Your holy fire flowing within our hearts, and our desire is that we shall be channels of Your Holy Spirit. We pray that You will take us ever more deeply into the shining glory of Your presence, that You will anoint us by Your Holy Spirit more and more intensely, and that a light shall be shone in every heart and a flame of revival kindle deeply within Your people. O Lord, we long for Your fire, we long for Your power. We long for Your flame of truth to ignite within our hearts, and a baptism of love for God come into every soul.*

O that there shall be a turning away from the dross, a turning away from carnality, a turning away from the trivia of this world, and that there will be a turning to You in reality and in truth, that we shall live as those who know that eternity is coming, that we shall live as though it were tomorrow that we should enter that eternal age. O let Your fire come down upon the sacrifice, let Your fire come down upon the altar, that, O Father, there shall be the reality of Your presence moving amongst us. Let Your holy flame ignite within us. Oh, the need for continuing revival in

the church of Christ, the need for a true
and a holy purpose to come into being
within us, that does away with
carelessness and foolishness.

Let there come, O Father, an
emptying out of rubbish and a coming
into being only of that which is real
gold. We ask You to do that which is
needful to bring us into this place of
singleness of purpose, singleness of
mission, singleness of vision. O holy
flame, come upon Your church! O holy
fire, come from above, and come into
the hearts of men and women all over
this land of Britain!

We pray too for a growing band who
will gather regularly already filled with
Your Holy Spirit and able to contribute
to the quality of our gatherings, rather
than waiting for others to bring the
sense of Your presence into the midst.
We pray, Lord, that living coals shall
come together, each from their own
quarter, alive, blazing with the fire of
Pentecost, and coming together to
contribute to that blazing fire which
shall touch the hearts of men. We pray,
Lord, that this shall come into being
swiftly, for we sense the need for a
growing band to bear the burden, to
carry responsibility, to be blazing
torches in the midst of the church of
Christ, and we ask You to bring us to
the place of sacrifice and reality that is
associated with revival. O Father,
deepen Your presence upon us, and
Your speaking in the midst of us, we
ask. Amen.

So when they had broken their fast, Jesus saith to Simon
Peter, Simon, son of John, lovest thou me more than these?
He saith unto him, Yea, Lord; thou knowest that I love
thee. He saith unto him, Feed my lambs. He saith to him
again a second time, Simon, son of John, lovest thou me?
He saith unto him, Yea, Lord; thou knowest that I love
thee. He saith unto him, Tend my sheep. He saith unto
him the third time, Simon, son of John, lovest thou me?
Peter was grieved because he said unto him the third time,
Lovest thou me? And he said unto him, Lord, thou know-
est all things: thou knowest that I love thee. Jesus saith
unto him, Feed my sheep (Jn 21:15–17).

A Shadow of Darkness

Frequently during the course of a week there come to
me various situations, questions and predicaments that
people get into. And sometimes as a result of the questions that rise I find that something particular may be
on my heart for preaching. During this last week there
were in fact quite a number of such interesting cases. I
won't go into great detail; but I give an example. One
gentleman had a brush with evil (deep, powerful evil)
in the life of another. This had shadowed him, and he
came to speak to me about it. I spoke of how to hold out
evil when encountered in this way, and prayed for the
lifting of the shadow. In the midst of our talk he suddenly turned to me and indicated that he did not know
how I was able to carry on the kind of work in which I
am involved, encountering evil. It touched a dimension
with which he felt he could not cope. He said, 'I
couldn't stand it.'

I replied, 'I don't stand it; I don't do anything. I am
merely there for God to move through. It's not a case of
fighting the devil. You move into Christ, and Christ
fights the devil.' My friend felt there must be an intoler-

able pressure because he knows that there is a constant stream of deep need coming all the time. There are evil powers from which people need deliverance, haunted houses, broken homes, and the agony that goes with all of these things. He suddenly found he was touching a dimension where he met that with which he just could not cope. I said, 'Well, I don't cope. That's the point: you don't cope. Christ copes.'

Like Plato, who was wont to lead his readers up the garden path, having them consider various possibilities and thoroughly entangling them and then saying in effect, 'That is not actually where we're going; it is somewhere else,' so may I say that that is not precisely where we are going now. It is somewhere else — although there is a thought connection.

The Seeing of Christ

Amongst the questions and the queries, there came one that caught my attention very particularly. It reminded me of something Miss Taylor used to speak of. People came to her for many reasons, but there was one reason in particular that thrilled her soul: when a person came to find more of Christ. Not just deliverance from some secret sin or powerful bondage, but a positive desire for the Lord Jesus. And I can understand that. The case that so caught my attention was of this kind. The person opened by saying, 'When you think of Christ, or you go through to Christ, do you see Him as a Person, or do you just have a general sense of His being there?' This opened up what to me is a fundamental and a profound subject. And I have felt a desire to take this up.

Now I am aware that again and again provision is being made for people who are at the beginning of their Christian lives, for people who are on the fringes, for people who are in great need, whether of spiritual deliverance or of physical healing or of baptism in the Holy Spirit. This is constant. But I felt that it is only right that those of you who want the highest heights and the deepest depths should at least occasionally have a measure of provision in the teaching that is given. I am moving into that dimension now, and I want you to follow carefully — I'll try to make this subject as understandable as I can, but that may not be easy, because when you are translating deep spiritual things into intellectual language it can be very difficult to transmit the meaning fully.

Shall I start with questioning you? When you pray, to whom do you pray? and what is your mental, visual, imagery when you pray? Ponder that for a moment. Christ has taught us to approach the Father in the Name of the Son, but we will all have different mental pictures of the Father as we make our petition.

What is your relationship with Christ, and how do you visualize Him? Does He have an appearance as in a physical form? Or is there just a general impression of a person? Or is there no visualization, and you have only a general feeling of spiritual well-being and spiritual light? Or do you not feel anything very much at all? Consider it for a moment.

What do you think it would be for these early disciples after Christ's death, resurrection and ascension? When they closed their eyes and they remembered Jesus, they would clearly remember a Person whom they had known, and had known intimately. He was Jesus the son of Mary, the Son of God, the One whom they had worshipped and loved. There would be no confusing of His Person with any other, or the memory of His face with any other. He was an individual with identity which was peculiarly His own. And they loved

Him. He was Jesus. They would remember Him vividly.

Now I have become aware as I have spoken to people that we are not all alike in our conception of Christ. There are those who have very strong powers of visualization. There are others who do not. I have to be careful, because I am fortunate in that I visualize very clearly, while some of you may not. I can see my earthly father's face as he lay in his coffin over sixty years ago, when I was about seven years of age; I can remember it now. I can remember faces very, very clearly. I could shut my eyes and picture some of you as clearly as though I were looking into your eyes. Indeed, it might surprise you to know that I could tell the colour of many of your eyes without looking at you. This is a family trait shared by one of my daughters: we tend to remember the colour of people's eyes when we have forgotten much else about them. I don't know quite why, but it just is so. There is a clear visual picture.

What is your picture of Jesus? When you draw near, do you have a vague idea of Christ's being there? Not delineated, just a feeling of well-being, without the seeing of a Person; or is there the consciousness of a Person with unique identity?

I am quite sure that the person who brought me the problem had a basic question in mind, which was this: 'Is there a dimension and a knowing of Christ that I have not yet entered, and is my sense of Christ too vague, too general? Is there something lacking?'

I am now turning that question on you. Is your relationship with Christ good and wholesome, but is there something lacking? In my view, in the vast majority of us there is a tremendous amount lacking. You say, 'What do you mean?'

Our Loving of Christ

Sometimes I find it is easy to get to a point in a negative way. And I want to say a little about my own experience here by way of illustration. In my early days, knowing about Christ, having been taught about Him, I discovered to my horror that I did not really like Him. That might shock you. You may have a very different background and have had a very different feeling. I respected Him; I admired Him; I would have given much to love Him — but I did not. I was honest, and I knew I did not. Indeed, His close presence made me feel very uncomfortable. You see, I was unsaved. I didn't know Him; I hadn't really met Him. He was a name and a figure, one who would cut off my sources of sin, and I found Him uncomfortable to be with, even at a distance.

There came a day when I found Christ. I was really born again. But, you know, even then I was not conscious of love. I was conscious of relief, joy that I had passed from death to life, but there was no real consciousness of love. Now let me warn you, we are all different, and don't judge too quickly because your experience may be different from mine. If I may refer again to Miss Taylor, I remember it was difficult for her to come to terms with the idea that I had found Christ but had not found a deep love for Christ. With her it was so different. In her early days she had turned against God because of bitterness, pain and difficulty in the family: her father died young, and one brother was badly injured. The young family came through a terrible time. One day she stood and looked out of her window and said in bitterness, 'God, I don't believe You exist. If there is a God, He is a monster.' Her soul went down into darkness and remained in darkness for years, till there came a night when, under the preaching of the late George Jeffreys in Greenock Town Hall, earth receded, the preacher receded, her friends receded, and she became intensely and painfully aware of God. She ultimately got home to her own apartment, and there, she said, the carpet became a pool of tears. Conviction of sin was upon her, and she knew the awfulness of being confronted by the living God against whom she had rebelled and whose very existence she had denied. He was there in that moment. In an agony, she knelt before Him. Suddenly in the mid-distance, between her and God, there arose a soft light: it was the light of Christ. Christ came to her and touched her, and found her. He placed on her the robe of His righteousness, and in a moment she passed from death to life. And, she said, 'I loved Him, I *loved* Him.' Ever after there was an intimacy and a fervour of love that I think I have never actually seen equalled on earth in any other. She loved Christ.

I didn't know her then, but the day came when I was in a gathering in which she was praying. Something happened in my soul. I didn't see her face, I didn't know her, knew almost nothing about her. Suddenly there opened in the heavens for me the knowledge of a love that could be between the soul and God of which I had never known. It came through her voice, it came through her imagery, it came through her prayer. I became intensely aware that there was a dimension of love for Christ that I had never known existed, and I have never forgotten it.

I had one experience prior to that which had given me some insight into love. I had come through a very painful experience, and when I had taken my cross and followed Him, in the hour of deepest pain He suddenly stood beside me: Jesus, the Son of God. I loved Him then for the first time in my life; I loved Him more than anybody on earth. In that one moment of time, in my need and distress and loneliness, He was there. But I did not know then of a dimension of love which could become the permanent home of the soul.

And so the days passed, the months passed, the years passed. I meet, and have met, many people, have heard many prayers that declare love for Christ. And I want to draw a distinction for you. I don't want to upset anybody by this distinction, but I want to draw it quite sharply and clearly. You can sit and think about Christ, and think about the love of Christ. You can think about loving Christ, and this can remain in your mind and be no more than a mental conception: a thinking about love. And indeed, you will find that if you want love to increase and you merely think about love it will diminish. But if you think on the object beloved it will grow; so with hatred. These don't feed on themselves: they feed on the objects loved or hated. Now it is my contention that while many of us talk about the love of Christ, and speak warmly of the love of Christ, and vocally express our love for Christ, there are very few who actually experience love in power.

Human Love

You say, 'What do you mean?' I've got to be careful about this — but I think it might give you a key if I take a human illustration. Take an ideal love between a young man and a young woman. Not merely sex-dominated, not just romantic moonlight, but a genuine, deep love relationship between the two. Circumstances cause them to be out of contact, and you are a go-between: you regularly meet and see both of them. Naturally both are anxious to hear from you: 'What did he say? What did she say? How did she react? What was she thinking? How did he look?' and so on. Each is anxious to get every detail of the beloved. There would come, however, a point where they would want you, the go-between, out of the way. They would desperately long to meet. Misunderstandings might have risen during the time spent apart, causing strain, unhappiness, vague suspicion. You can imagine the meeting. The detail of the misunderstanding would take second place. They would want that sorted, no doubt, but deep down there would be something more important. They would want to know the fundamental truth: 'Tell me, do you love me? Do I have your heart? Do you belong to me? Am I yours?' We do not have too much difficulty in understanding this dimension of human love.

The Mystery of Christ's Love

But when I leave human love aside and say, 'Come up higher, to the relationship between Christ and the soul,' should that cause any difficulty? Do you realize that He wants you to love Him more than any human lover ever loved a beloved? He wants that love personally. For His part, He loves you more than any human lover ever loved a beloved, and He wants you to experience that love, and to live in the power and the joy of it. He wants to lavish His love upon you, and He in turn wants to enjoy your love. Now I do understand why this can be very difficult for people, very difficult indeed. Immediately a person may draw back and say, 'But what could Christ ever get of value from me? What is the worth of my puny love?' What can it matter to the Creator of the ends of the earth that a worm of the dust should say, 'I love you'? 'So what?' is how some of you might react. And I think that the scripture that I have read to you tonight is one of the most amazing ever penned. Stand back from it for a little. Peter had broken in the hour of desperate trial and denied Christ with oaths and curses, indeed bitterly denied Him. Having previously been warned by Christ that before the cock crowed twice he would deny Him thrice, he still denied Him. Suddenly the cock crowed and he remembered. I imagine him lifting his eyes and looking into the eyes of the Son of God, and the eyes of the Son of God looking into Peter. What a moment! He went out, and he wept bitterly. Who was Peter? What was the significance of one man? If you take the total population of earth that lived before and after Peter, to say that one man was as the fine dust in the balance is to give him a size that is far out of proportion. If you said he was like a grain of sand on the seashore, you might be nearer the truth. Small dust, Peter: a small grain, Peter. In the presence of the Son of God who was God the Son, the Creator of all worlds, where did Peter figure? Of Christ we read that *without him hath not anything been made that hath been made* (Jn 1:3). He upheld the very cross on which He was crucified. In Him all things consist. They have their cohesion through the Lord Jesus Christ, all things, all the rolling stars in space, all the vast galaxies — the whole vast universe. All was created by Jesus.

To Simon, who was a worm of the dust, He said, 'Do you love Me?' Do you hear, Simon, what Christ is saying to you?

May I paraphrase: 'Simon, don't you understand? It is important to Me that you should love Me. It is of tremendous importance to Me that you should love Me. It is so important to Me that I died for you on the cross. Don't you begin to understand the depth of My love for you, Simon?'

Peter, can you comprehend that? I can't comprehend that. I believe it, but I don't understand it. 'He wants my love — my puny love. He wants the affection of my heart. What can it matter to the Son of God whom I love, what I do with my life?' Friend, I don't understand it, but I know it's true, and I know that as men and women begin to follow the Nazarene, they too take on His nature, and they love others for His sake. And they break their hearts for the salvation of others, as His Spirit enters into them. The passion of the cross comes upon the hearts of men, and we enter into the nature of the Son of God. And I want to get right to the heart of this great truth.

It is important that you should work for God. It is important that you should think about Christ. But you know, you could work for God to the end of your days, and think about Christ to the end of time, and still deny Him that one thing that He wants so desperately — if I might use that word reverently in connection with Christ, and I believe I may. He wants your love. It is as though He says, 'Put your work aside. Put your thinking aside. Sit down, and give Me your love. Shut the door, shut everybody else out. Shut your work out — your work for Me, shut it out. I want you, and I want you to receive Me. I want to become one being with you in an aloneness into which no other will ever enter.' That is the union with Christ. You will find the great Christian mystics speak about union with God. And the vast majority of mankind stay outside the door and they don't understand for one moment what such mystics are talking about. The mystics are, however, talking truth: they are at the heart of the universe. Love for God: God is love, God is light. In love He created, in love He sent His Son. *For God so loved the world, that he gave his only begotten son* (Jn 3:16). *Beloved, let us love one another: for love is of God* (1 Jn 4:7). Go through the Bible, and you will find a powerful emphasis on love. You say, 'But I wanted to work for God. I wanted to do something for God.' Find Christ in this deep, deep union, and you will have more to do for God than you can even begin to imagine. Work flows out from relationship, not relationship from work. Make Christ central.

Effects of Love

In Scotland, love is a word that we don't overwork. We don't like to wear our hearts too obviously on our sleeves. Some of us can conceal our feelings so deeply that others may wonder if we have hearts at all! I know that males, especially young males, admire courage and strength, aggression, toughness. Words like peace and love leave them remarkably cold. They tend to grow up that way. The early prejudice against soft words can remain. You know, this is so very foolish. Love is at the foundation of life. Ideally, even at a natural level, life should be conceived in love — never merely the result of a loveless sexual function. Love is at the very foundation of human life.

I have told many of you before of that discovery by the psychologists that when children were neglected in a big institution and treated almost as being without identity, their mortality rate was very high: far higher than average. The IQ level, too, was very low. In a smaller institution where the children were given individual love and attention, the IQ was much higher and mortality much lower.

In the deeps of spiritual life, if you don't love people, they will know it and respond accordingly. If you who are leaders of groups and churches don't really love, your work will suffer. It's a strange thing; I don't always understand this, but people know very quickly if you

care for them. You might have a gruff exterior, and do
little but insult them in a Scottish way, but if at the
deep levels you really love them, they will know it. I
don't know how they know, but they do know — oh,
yes, they know. Many years ago, in a time of conflict, it
was drawn to my attention by one young man that
although there was little vocalizing of love it didn't
mean the love wasn't there. If people are cared for they
know it and respond in kind. Love is not just something we think about. It is a felt thing. You may present
a false front, but if you are unreal people will know it;
hypocrisy will out. You may speak honeyed words and
make no impact. You may speak a gruff couple of
sentences, but if you care for people they will sense it.
You may not be complimenting them, but the true
feeling transmits in the air, in the atmosphere: he cares,
she cares. I don't know how this is so clearly picked up,
but picked up it is, and no camouflage will do. You
must have the real thing. And that real thing is born in
depth in aloneness with Christ. You put on Christ. You
let Him grow in you, and His love grows within you. As
He cares for others you begin to care with His care. And
this care is exceedingly infectious.

Alone with God

I'll come back now to the central question. When you
are in that aloneness, what do you see? What do you
feel? I can't speak for others; our experiences are so
individual. But this I do know, that when the soul is
right with God there is, to begin with, a general feeling
of the presence of God. At that point nothing may be
particularized. There is just a feeling of God. You can
get that in a good meeting. But there can come a point
when you move from a general feeling of divine pres-

ence and spiritual well-being to the contemplation of the Person of Christ as an individual, and you allow yourself to go out to Him and be totally one with Him. This time of aloneness is, I suggest, more important to Him than it may appear to be to you. He is calling you in there to have tryst with God, to have tryst with Christ. If you loved someone deeply with a human love, and you were longing to be alone with them, and they turned up for the engagement bringing another with them, how would you feel? If they said, 'We thought we'd have a very happy time all together,' it wouldn't be happy for you.

When you love Christ, and really feel His love, there is a place in the soul for total isolation from all on earth. I have known a person come seeking the baptism in the Spirit, and a boyfriend has come over and embraced her. That upsets me greatly if I am the person ministering. I am quite capable of taking an embracing arm and putting it elsewhere, but if I feel the circumstances are such that that will be too hurtful, I try to sit between the couple, and that prevents any further nonsense! There is no place for that kind of sentiment in the deep places of the soul with God. You are alone. You are not complete in some other and then in Christ. You are complete in Christ, and the overflow of that completion can go out to others, which is a very different matter: complete in Christ.

Do not take your inhibitions in there. Do not take your shyness. Do not take your disinclination to be expressive in there. Be in the aloneness and pour out your love, and let it grow. Let your love develop, and don't think it's a sentimental thing: it is, I might say, of the very essence of life: it is near to the very foundation of true life. Let love grow.

You say, 'How?'

Practical Steps

Merely to sit and think about it will not in itself help it to grow one iota. I give the following instruction all across the country, and have done so for many years. Take fifteen minutes each day. I don't say an hour, because for many people an hour is an eternity. Take fifteen minutes. Read about Jesus for five minutes; shut your Bible; for the next five minutes go over in your mind what you have read until it is clear before you. Perhaps you will see Him healing the sick, preaching to the multitude, speaking to the woman at the well — it doesn't really matter where. First read, then ponder. In the third five minutes, turn your eyes to look directly to Him, and love Him. Your mind may try to wander away: bring it back. Love Him. Let the fullness of your heart go out to Him. Love Him without embarrassment, without inhibition. Rejoice in your love, glory in your love, enjoy your love. Move into a realm of ecstasy in Jesus Christ your Lord, and you will come out from that inner place, that union of the soul with God, deeply affected. You will move in a new dimension, and your work will move into another dimension from the one that many of you have known. From your life there will be an emanation of Christ.

Do you realize that with souls like Madame Guyon, for example,

> All scenes alike engaging prove
> To souls imprest with sacred love;
> Where'er they dwell, they dwell in Thee,
> In heav'n, in earth, or on the sea.

Whether she was in a palace or in a prison, it made no difference to her, for she had come to a position in life that wherever she was, Christ was. And wherever

Christ was, Heaven was. The prison cell became veritable Heaven because she dwelt in God. Man had no more power over her, because she was in that dimension with God. That is not for a few of the elect: that is the birthright of the church of Jesus Christ. Christ is calling for lovers.

Love that Breaks the Heart

'Simon: are you not bitterly repentant of the sin you committed? Are you not ashamed of what you have done? Simon, what hope have you of working for Me for the rest of your life? You are a shame to the church: who will ever believe in you, Simon? Simon, in My great grace I am letting you into the kingdom of Heaven by the skin of your teeth.'

Are these the words of Jesus? No, never! He said not a word of Peter's treachery, not a word of his oaths and curses, not a word of his denials, not a word of His previous warning, but: 'Simon, tell Me, do you love Me?'

Jesus, pleading for the love of man. 'Yea, Lord, Thou knowest that I love Thee.' You say, 'That's what it's like with a lot of us. Of course we love Jesus.' Oh, yes, it's on many a lip — 'Oh yes, I love Christ.' That can be easily said, but may not be a profession of real love at all. It can be no more than parrot talk.

'Simon: do you really love Me?'

'It doesn't look like it, after what I've done, does it? I am guilty. But yes, I do love You.'

I believe there is more depth in the second answer. Simon has been more deeply probed.

'Simon, son of John, do you really love Me — do you passionately love Me?'

'Lord, You know all things. See into my heart: You know.'

Get there now. 'See into my heart with all its puny love, strong love, whatever love, and come into my heart in such a way that there is no room for any other in all the world. Fill me with Yourself, Lord, fill me with Yourself.'

Ultimate Goals

I opened to you earlier what a man could be in Christ: like Christ in his generation. And it was a noble conception, a glorious theme. Now I am opening to you a further aspect of the same theme: being a lover of Christ. He can be for you the Lover of your soul. You can go out in an ecstasy, and you can live largely in an ecstasy, and some of the saints of God do live largely in ecstasy (although they have intense trials as well). I will say this too. There are times in that inner realm when your access is deeper than at others. The devil will try to shade your vision and to hold you out from that deepest depth. But don't allow it. Don't be content with finding Christ in the outer courts, as it were. Press through into the inmost sanctuary where you see Him in spirit face to face.

Invitation

If you have felt the Holy Spirit touch you and put in you a warm and a godly ambition to become a lover of Christ in a realm that you have never known, and to a depth that you have never known, then respond. Realize that there is the opening of a door by the Holy One. It is a thing that God does. Open your heart, open the door. *Behold, I stand at the door and knock: if any man hear my voice and open the door, I will come in to him, and will sup with him, and he with me* (Rev 3:20). Oh, the glory of being loved of Christ: not merely thinking about love, but actually feeling it. It is wonderful, when you are in need, to meet someone and suddenly feel the warmth of their love coming to you, not a weak, sentimental sensation, but real, deep, wonderful love that can transmit from human to human. Move into that in the realm of the divine. Blessed be His Name.

> PROPHECY: *Surely You have opened Heaven and the cloud of Your glory has dropped its sweetness down from Heaven upon us, and our spirit is saturated in that loveliness, and our soul is anchored to that life within the veil, through the Lord Jesus Christ. There is no other way, there is no other place to be, there is no other centre for the sustenance of the soul, there is no other desire within the heart finding its way up that narrow road into the glory of the light, into the place where God Himself is, and there is no other voice save the voice of the Beloved: held captive by His love. And from that place there issues forth a fountain of love between the soul and Christ, and between the soul and others in Christ. For sometimes He takes one and another into that life of separation, where Christ becomes the home of the soul, and in His infinite wisdom He brings the cloud of glory that surrounds one life into touch with the cloud of glory that He has placed around another. And the two clouds meet and merge, and the intensity of the shining of the glory and the coming forth of the rays of His light upon others is accordingly increased. Do not fight when the Holy Spirit reveals this way of love. His work is perfect, and His ways in the heart of a man are revealed. Be blessed of the Lord in your going and in your coming, in your downsitting and in your uprising, for, beloved, you*

*will have what your heart truly seeks, and if you
seek for bread, will I give to you a stone?**

---

* The tape on which this prophecy was being recorded ran out at this
point.

4 | BEYOND FORGIVENESS TO LOVE

EXHORTATION AND PRAYER [MB]: *Our hearts are filled with joy as we come to You, and already Your presence is all round us. You are showing us the ways of the most high God, You are showing us the way into the holy place, You are showing us Your ways of holiness. Our hearts warm toward You as we gaze upon the Christ, having the satisfaction of knowing that He is here, and that He is inside us, and we are partakers of His glory — that satisfaction enters into our being, and we give You praise. As there is a rising of worship, as there is a giving of glory, as there is a praising of the most high God by the multitude, surely the air becomes filled with Your presence. A door is opened wide before us into spiritual places, into the very kingdom of the most high God, into the very kingdom of Heaven itself. Oh, glory be unto You, Lord God of Hosts! A shout goes up from the camp, hallelujah! Glory and praise unto You, O God of Hosts! The door is opened: swing wide the gates, swing wide the doors, that the King of Glory may enter in.*

O yes, swing wide the gates for the entrance of the King of Glory, that He

> *may come forth with triumphant
> chords, that He may come with
> triumphant sound, and His angels with
> Him. Oh, let Your glory come down to
> man, let the fullness of Your presence,
> the presence of revival, break through!*
>
> *O arise and shine, for your light is
> come, and the glory of the Lord has
> risen upon you. Arise through the gates,
> arise into the glory of high
> Heaven...Lift Him up for the world to
> see. All praises in the highest, hosanna
> in the highest, all glory in the highest.*

My readings are from the epistle of Paul to the Romans:

For I know that in me, that is, in my flesh, dwelleth no good thing: for to will is present with me, but to do that which is good is not. For the good which I would I do not, but the evil which I would not, that I practise. But if what I would not, that I do, it is no more I that do it, but sin which dwelleth in me. I find then the law, that, to me who would do good, evil is present. For I delight in the law of God after the inward man: But I see a different law in my members, warring against the law of my mind, and bringing me into captivity under the law of sin which is in my members. O wretched man that I am! who shall deliver me out of the body of this death? I thank God through Jesus Christ our Lord (Rom 7:18–25).

For they that are after the flesh do mind the things of the flesh; but they that are after the spirit the things of the spirit. For the mind of the flesh is death; but the mind of the spirit is life and peace: Because the mind of the flesh is enmity against God; for it is not subject to the law of God, neither indeed can it be: And they that are in the flesh cannot please God (Rom 8:5–8).

And I would add to these two readings another word: *I am crucified with Christ; yet I live; and yet no longer I, but Christ liveth in me* (Gal 2:20).

Going On from First Principles

From time to time I feel it is right for me to strike a deeper teaching note even on an outreach occasion. Many services are largely given over to the interests of newcomers (I don't mean visitors; I mean newcomers in the sense of people who have not yet come deeply into the life of Christ, who are in a position and condition which require elementary instruction). The preaching is suited to their needs. Again and again God meets us at that level, and people are delivered from evil power, they are healed from physical sickness, they are baptized in the Holy Spirit. These are wonderful events, and long may they continue. But there is another area where people have passed from the first principles of Christ, and are entering into deeper waters. At this point there can be a real struggle, as we find reflected in our reading from Paul. It is to the latter group that my preaching is now addressed.

In a strange way the background of this study is very similar to the background of the previous study. Remember the emphasis there on the love of God and on the relationship of the soul with God, a relationship of love. The theme arose from a question that had been put to me about the visualization of Christ, and the importance of personal relationship with Christ in the deepening of spiritual life. This present address also stems from a question, or rather a situation that came before me involving one of you who is experiencing deep and prolonged suffering. As I pondered the issues, I very quickly realized that the matter could profitably be brought in principle before a wider audience. And I could scarcely believe it when someone else approached me with a very similar problem: the detail was quite different, but the deep principle was almost identical. I then thought of a number of other people in the same category known to me. There are five cases before me, and in all five the same basic problem has surfaced.

I want to be very careful in my teaching. One can be too theoretic in teaching, and God wants to bring us from vague theory into the realm of practice and reality. Let me explain what I mean. Many of you know the theory of the doctrine of death to self very well. You know that it is the will of God that we should reckon ourselves dead at a mind level, at a heart level, and in the realm of the will. In all of these realms we should be dead to self, with only the life of Christ flowing through us. The old man and his works should be cast off, and the new man after Christ Jesus should be in the ascendant within us. You know the teaching: if you feed the old man, he will grow; if you starve him, he will tend to die. If you feed the new man, he will grow, and if you starve him, he will fade. The theory is very well known by many of you. You may grasp the theory, and by grasping the theory think that you have grasped the truth. What in fact you have grasped is the theory of the truth, as distinct from the experience of the truth.

When it comes to the realm of practice, it can be so terribly different from the realm of theory. This could be illustrated at various levels, but perhaps one or two examples will suffice for the moment. At the heart level, a person who understands the theory can find him/herself in a romantic attachment, knowing deep down that this is not the will of God. This is not the girl for me, this is not the boy of God's choice. But the heart is involved, and the affections of the heart are capti-vated. The actual renunciation of something wrong, the crucifixion of the heart, is a very difficult thing to do. Hudson Taylor did it with tremendous benefit. Many another has refused to do it, and has been the poorer for a lifetime as a result.

In the realm of the will, though you may know quite well that God's will for you is a particular thing, it doesn't suit you, you are not prepared to do it, and you rebel. You know the theory, but the outworking of the theory is a different matter; it means discipline over detailed things: not only the broad sweep, as it were, but the detail of life.

And so we come to our five problem cases.

Passing from Forgiveness to Love

In the first case there was a clear knowledge of the teaching that we must forgive, as Christians. A lady had been wronged on a particular issue quite a long time back and had genuinely forgiven the person concerned, but realized that there was a shadow over the matter which had never gone away. From her point of view there had been injustice and misunderstanding, but basically she felt that she had been wronged. She felt she had forgiven, but the shadow remained.

Case number two concerns an individual who finds herself at present in very serious, difficult situations, facing mindless violence, often resulting from drug abuse. She is prepared for Christ's sake to do the Christlike thing, albeit with difficulty.

Case number three involves exceedingly cruel, hor-rible treatment by a stepfather, with a cruelty that is ongoing.

Case number four concerns bitterness and hatred in a

lady's life because of the way her father had treated her mother.

Case number five concerns bitterness against a father for the cruelty of his treatment to his son in his early days.

There you have five cases, and there is a sense in which they are one case, because they bring into sharp relief a particular principle, and raise the fundamental question of what a Christian should do in such circumstances.

In all five cases the people concerned had already reached a position of forgiveness, real forgiveness — not just a profession of it or merely a willingness to forgive. To each of them I told my own personal experience, of which I have previously both spoken and written. Let me go over it again, for it is of vital significance.

God Teaches the Lesson

I started (as I am sure many of you have done) with a strong, unbroken will, determination to get my own way, to do my own thing, to be under nobody's control. If somebody crossed me, I had the kind of temperament to take revenge. I was not the kind to take insults lightly or lying down. I began to seek God, and was genuinely seeking Him deeply, having a background knowledge of the teachings of consecration and holiness. Suddenly a man wronged me, and wronged me very badly from my point of view. He said unjustified things, he was jealous of something that I had — I was enraged, and I had it in my heart to fix him, as the Americans would say, real good. And not only did I have it in my heart: I had it in my power to do it, because of information to which I was privy (whether true or rumour I am not quite sure, but it could have been badly used).

I remember so clearly (it is strange how details become imprinted on one's mind), I was at my folks' farm, carrying two pails of swill to the piggery to feed the pigs. And as I walked, God spoke to me. You know, lots of people are snobs, but God doesn't mind whether you are carrying swill or mucking out byres. Some of the loveliest times I've ever had with God were in these kinds of circumstance. The neighbours weren't always too keen when you went in with smelly boots, but God never minded.

He spoke to me very clearly concerning the one at whom I was enraged. He said, 'I love that man.' I didn't want to hear anything about that, and I just shut my ears and trudged on with my two pails of swill. I hadn't gone very far when He spoke again. (Now I am trying to give you it as accurately as I remember it: it isn't always easy to keep the close detail accurate.)

'Do you think that you are better than Christ, that you have a right to hate that man?'

That stopped me, stopped me right in my tracks. I don't mean it stopped my feet — I went on walking — but it stopped me in my spirit.

Then God did for me a very wonderful thing. He let me know that He did not expect me to love the evil in that man. But it was as though He showed me that he was a shoddy creature, and He showed me the kind of man He wanted him to be in Christ — and you know, I could love the second. My love went out to what God wanted him to be. All sense of injustice and bitterness passed away, and I knew the love of Christ for that man.

The months and the years passed, and one day he came to me. His son was having a bad deal from a headmaster. The father explained the position and asked my advice as to what he should do — because his lad's career was about to be ruined. I said, 'There's no problem. I'll dictate a letter or tell you what to write yourself. Address it to the Director of Education, and you will find the matter will be sorted.' Basically the head teacher was preventing the boy taking certain subjects that he required in a particular combination to be sure of university entrance. Within forty-eight hours the matter was sorted: the Director dealt with it immediately. You know, that man was exceedingly grateful. It changed the whole course of a life, and surely was a much better outcome for me than the getting of a cheap revenge at an earlier stage. I thought this was good; I had learned something.

And Again at a Deeper Level

Watch and you will often find that God teaches you more than one lesson on the same subject; we often need more than one lesson. On this matter God dealt with me in three distinct stages. The years passed, and I was baptized in the Holy Spirit; it was a wonderful experience. It was quickly followed by persecution. At the time I was living in town and working on a farm. I had to travel up country each day. I had a dog to which I was very deeply attached. One day for some reason I left him at home, but he managed to escape. He then set out to trudge four or five miles up into the country to find me. Two men found him, and shot him...on the ground that there was danger of sheep-worrying. Now my nature is such that if that had happened at an earlier time I should not like to think what I might have done. I have always had a love for dogs in general, never mind a dog that was my own particular friend. Immediately God spoke to me. At that time I was going into deeps with God; it was in our early days, when Miss Taylor was very much used amongst a small group of us who used to meet regularly. I knew that if I gave way to the bitterness, anger and hatred that could have so easily welled up, I would be shutting the door on something of infinite worth. By God's grace I put the grievance away as though it had never happened, and I never allowed a trace of bitterness to touch my spirit. And God stood by me.

You say, 'Well, surely that was you through.'

I might at the time have said, 'Yes, I think that's true. I think I'm through on this now.'

A Third and Victorious Stage

The days passed, persecution deepened. There was one who was in a position to exercise real power, and I was suffering intensely. When things were at their worst, I remember going into my bedroom alone and kneeling down at the bedside. I took a grip and came to the place where I was able honestly to say, 'I forgive him.' And it was as though God immediately said, 'I'm not interested in your forgiveness.' I was quite shocked. He said, 'I want you to love him.' That was just too much. All the natural, human part of me would have loved him at the end of a stick. God said, 'Love him.' I was not willing, but I *was* willing to be made willing. I bowed my head, and I opened my spirit to obey the command of God. Immediately the love of God flooded my heart, and I loved that man with a deep, deep love, the love of God. In a moment, all his power to hurt, all his power over me, was gone. It broke in that moment of time, and it never came again. I had obtained the victory. *This is the victory that overcometh the world*: the love of God. Please note this: I was never fully through on this issue until I loved my enemy. Forgiveness was not enough.

Love was absolutely vital. I had to love him, and God made love possible. If we *do not* love, it is because we *will not* love.

Five Cases of Injustice

And now we return to the five cases. The first lady realized that it could be very difficult to go to where God wanted her to go if there was no clearing of the shadow which still persisted. I showed her that forgiveness is not enough. In every such situation you have to love. When you have been seriously, unjustly dealt with, cruelly maligned, without recompense, without apology, without restitution of any kind, Christ wants you to love.

The second case was very similar. You are not expected to love the evil man under the power of drugs who would kill you, but you are expected to see with the eyes of Christ the poor, wretched creature whom He loves in spite of his sordidness and his sin.

In the third case, I so clearly remember that when the lady concerned faced her problem and took Christ's way, she came into a glorious liberation. She had been treated with desperate injustice and continuous cruelty. There came a moment when there was true forgiveness, and with the flowing of love her spirit was set totally free.

In the fourth case, when the person heard what I had to say, the tears flowed down her cheeks, and a spirit of hatred and bitterness came welling out. She was set free with the freedom of Christ, as was the young man who hated his father.

In the fifth case, when the hatred and aggression were put away they were replaced by love.

These victories are not gained in some high ivory

tower remote from life. These victories are gained right where you are in the midst of sordidness, and they are gained when you are up against hell coming through other individuals.

The Earthly and the Heavenly Planes

You see, if I may put it very directly to you, there are two planes. There is the earthly plane, and there is the heavenly. When you judge at an earthly level, you see the injustices, you feel the resentment, you experience the bitterness, you know the power of hatred — and who could easily criticize you, saying that these things are not so? You are seeing real situations and are giving human judgments. You are at the receiving end of the injustices, and understandably you have attendant emotions. Now that is according to the law of the flesh, the law that applies to the 'old man', as the Bible describes us in our fallen condition. But a new law has come into our hearts with Christ, and He wants us now not to judge with the old law, but with the new law, with Christ's judgment. Christ looks at these situations with a view to heal, and not only to heal the delinquent, the perpetrator of the injustice, but in a more subtle sense to heal you — because you drink poison when you react with hatred and bitterness. He takes the poison away, and He gives you the flow of divine love.

Horrors of Injustice and Evil

As I pondered these things, my spirit went out beyond the first case, beyond the five cases, and roamed the world with its present international pains and problems. I saw again, as no doubt you have seen in your daily papers, an old man lying badly wounded on a street of Sarajevo: a poor old man, who probably had nothing to do with the conflict. I remembered reading of a shell bursting amongst a group of civilians and killing many of them. I recalled the horrors in Yugoslavia: the dead amongst the Croats, amongst the Serbs, the conflict in Bosnia-Herzegovina, the awful cruelty, the death toll, the injustice. My spirit went to Somalia: about five hundred a day are dying there of starvation. You will have seen the pictures: children, rickles of bones; adults, scarecrows; dying in the agony of hunger, in a world where there is plenty of food. Do you think that no thoughts of injustice rise within their breasts? Some of them have never known anything else: they have been starving since their earliest days. Is there no room for bitterness, hatred?

If it was happening here, if our dear ones were killed in a quarrel in which we had no real concern, would we have no strong reactions? If people were being butchered in our locality as in Northern Ireland for no good reason, shot down, killed, tortured, how would we feel? The murdered victims pass before our eyes in the press day by day; in a recent case a young man just clobbered another from behind and killed him. He did not even know him; there was no real reason for his action; he just felt like doing it. If you were the victim's father, mother, fiancée, wife, would you have no bitterness? You have to face that. No bitterness? No hatred?

Closing Our Lips

As I look round at the sea of human sin and at the depth of the injustice and the cruelty and the violence, I say, 'O God — O God, I can't speak glib words to a company, to tell them just to be rid of all these negative feelings.' Negative feelings, did I say? *Negative* feelings? *Hatred*, and *anger*, with tremendous justification at a natural level! Just imagine it, your nearest and dearest slaughtered for no reason in this wide world. Again I know: I had a brother who was murdered in the prime of life for no good reason. And if you had said to me in these days, 'What is your attitude to the man who murdered him?' I might have said, 'If we meet one dark night, one of us may not go on living.' I actually used to ponder this. I knew what it was to have lost a brother and, although I was still a boy, if I had attacked his killer and was going down cruelly I would have fought, I think, to the last drop of my blood. I know what human feelings are.

I viewed the international scene — in Russia, in Pakistan, the Kurds, the Shi'ite Muslims in the south of Iraq, the borders of Israel — all over, people dying unjustly. What has Christianity to say about all that? Are you going to give a glib formula and say, 'Well, just tell them to forgive'? No, I am not going to do that. I do not have the right to do that.

A Still Greater Injustice

But I am going to tell you something else. I am going to take you to a worse injustice than any I have mentioned, greater than all of them rolled together. One day, there appeared on earth a man who did nothing but good. His every act was based on love. He healed the sick, He raised the dead, He fed the multitudes, He showed a way that men had never seen before. And men took Him, and gave Him one of the cruellest deaths that is known to man — because crucifixion tortures the body in many ways at the same time. No one of the excruciating pains results in a quick death, but the combination of agonies is horrendous.

And Christ's Response

I pictured the Lord Jesus hanging on that cross, and I pictured Him saying to the crowd around the cross: 'I healed your sick, I raised your dead, I fed your multitudes. I have obeyed the will of God in every particular. I have loved you with an everlasting love. And now you have put Me on this cross. Father, forgive them: they know not what they do.' His love rose superior to His sufferings. The most cruelly mistreated person who ever lived, loved in His deepest pain, in His darkest hour, and won a world through love. I have no right to say to the weeping, tortured souls of earth, 'Forgive and love,' in the way that He has. It is as though He leans down and He says,

'Look, I have felt it all. I am able to be with you in your dark hour now. I have gone that way. I have gone the way of the cross, and there is no worse way than the way of the cross. I have suffered all that you suffer, I have known all that you know of pain. And the way of hatred and revenge will land you in further, in eternal pain. There is a door of escape: I opened the door for all mankind. It is the door of love, and all who find Me and go that way are overcomers. They triumph. Let your hearts be full of love, and you will have power over all the power of the enemy, and you will live and die in glory as I lived and died and went into the glory of God.'

What of You?

I am asking you, what are your paltry grievances, your little hatreds and your bitternesses, your sense of injustices? I am asking you to make a bundle of them, and bow before the cross of Jesus Christ. Pass the point where you say, 'Father, forgive them,' and reach the point where Christ dwelt: love them, love those who have done and are doing you evil even now. You will find that this is the outworking of sanctification and the fulfilment of the law of death to self. Come down from the clouds of theory and put it in practice until you haven't one thing in your heart against any man or woman born. Love them for Christ's sake. This is the law of Christ, this is the law of sanctification, this is the law of love. To fail in it makes us hypocrites, Christian hypocrites. I say it again: if you don't reach that high standard, you are a Christian hypocrite, for this is the clear law of Christ, and it brooks no argument. Don't ask for justice, lest you get it and perish: ask for mercy, and live forever. Do not expect justice; but love you can assuredly have. Blessed be the name of the Lord.

A Hard Saying

I know this isn't the easiest teaching in the world. I know that there are those with itching ears who would heap to themselves teachers and hear them say pleasant things, such as, 'You are a fine lot of people!' Now, to be quite honest, I don't think that we are very fine people. I think that by and large we are deplorable people. But even so we were sufficiently important for Christ to die for us. He loves us, and He is beginning to make something of some of us. Don't look for compliments: look for truth. In receiving truth you will get blessing, and the close, near, glorious presence of the living God, who seeks truth in the inner parts. Blessed be the name of the Lord.

> PRAYER: *The theory of these things is so easy, so rational, so understandable. And the moment we understand and make the mistake of thinking that as a result we have received, we need to be careful,*

Lord, lest You put us through a test, to show to us just how deep or how shallow our love really is, and whether we have grasped the eternal truth. Lord, we pray tonight that there will be those who will know the wonderful experience of the great attraction of the way of Christ, who will experience the expulsive power of a greater affection.

We pray that there may be those who are ambitious for God; who want to reach the highest heights and who suddenly realize that these heights are unattainable unless we become Christlike and put this kind of teaching into literal practice, accepting it not just in theory but in reality. This is the road up. Lord, let us become so taken with the vision glorious, the potential that there is in Christ, that for His sake and for the sake of the vision we will discard all thoughts of revenge and injustice and fighting for our rights, and move on to that higher plane where Christ is, that we may dwell in Him, and He in us.

Lord, we pray that those to whom You are speaking will come to that point where they will do something about it.

Invitation

I am asking those of you to whom Christ has spoken and who have carried hidden sores and pains and wounds, many of which may have seemed justified, to give them over to God. You want to come up higher to where another law prevails: the law of love, the law of Christ. If you are prepared to do that, I would like to bring you to a point of commitment. Respond now to the Son of God.

PRAYER: *Lord, we pray for every one, for there is a point of commitment, but there is also a point where You come in and work the miracle. We pray that it shall be so now. We ask it in Christ's name and for His sake.*

PRAYER [MB]: *We give honour unto You, for You are the glorious King of Kings and the Lord of Lords, and Your power has touched us; the anointing of Your Holy Spirit has come down to show us Jesus, to show us the perfection of His loveliness, to show us the glory that lies on ahead of us, to show us the power and the beauty of the mind of the Lord Jesus Christ. We are sailing toward that glory, into that wonderful horizon of light, and a panorama of riches is opening before our gaze. Surely, O God, You would have us come on to higher ground, You would have us reach into that glorious place where we are truly anointed and directed by the Spirit, where the wonderful, unsearchable riches of the Godhead are opened to us in the Lord Jesus Christ. O the sea of glory, O the wonderful panorama of light. Surely, Lord,* Higher up and further in, *is always Your call upon us, never to settle for the level we are at, but always to reach out to that further horizon, to that higher height, where Your glory dominates and prevails, where all barriers are swept away, where the things of time become as nothing, where the things in our own lives that are hindrances become small molehills of no account, and our deficiency is met in Your sufficiency. O wonderful, wonderful glory of God, wonderful opening into spiritual places. A door is opened in the heavenlies, a door is opened which no man can shut.*

5 | BEYOND ACCEPTANCE TO REJOICING

The experience in which I moved from forgiveness to love was like the explosion of a bomb in my life. It was not temporary, nor for that occasion alone, but permanent. I was never the same again. Something critical, vital and lifelong happened in that hour. I entered another dimension, and I had an experimental knowledge of a vital spiritual principle. I realized that my feelings of injustice and resentment were small matters, and through passing from mere forgiveness of the person concerned to positively loving him, I had come into a place where the very life of God and the love of God throbbed in me, and the power and the life and the love all went together.

A Place of Pain

Strangely enough, I met someone else recently who has given me permission to tell the following story, which illustrates another very similar spiritual principle — God's demand, or perhaps I should say the opportunity God extends to us, of passing from the place of the mere acceptance of His will in painful circumstances to the place of positively rejoicing in the situation.

My friend had been reading Hannah Hurnard's book,

Hind's Feet in High Places, and it had been powerfully speaking to him. This man had come through a very difficult time — not just for an hour or a week or a month; he was in a family situation that had involved incredible hurt over years, pain and suffering such as few of us ever face. I always move very carefully when I am dealing with things like that. I do not give glib advice. Similarly when dealing with another's illness I am deeply conscious that if I am in health it is not very helpful to put my hand on the sufferer's shoulder and say heartily, 'Well, buck up, friend, and adopt a good, positive attitude! Things will get better.' It's all very well for me to be cheerful if I am in health, but it is not very helpful to a person who is deeply suffering. I find the same at times of death. Rather than speak glib words, I like to have words that come from God, words that are real. I do not like cheap dealing. When I surveyed the position of my friend, cruelly alienated from people he loved, I knew the horror of it. I had one very short period in the course of a lifetime when I suffered a little in this way, but enough to give me an insight into the kind of situation that my friend has known for years.

How do you have hind's feet in high places? How do you skip upon the mountains like a gazelle, when you are carrying such weight, such pain? There is a line from a famous song which indicates the difficulty of jumping up high with the devil on your back. This gives cause for thought. You can be so pressed by your circumstances, so bleeding with unbearable pain, that there is a shadow on your whole life. As I talked to my friend I suddenly saw something in a way I had never really quite seen it before. I knew he had come to terms with accepting the will of God in the situation, and I believe there will probably be many of you who have had your own individual problems with which you have come to terms. You have accepted the will of God, and you have accepted the pain that goes with the circumstances as a cross that you must carry. A shadow is there and you expect it to remain because you are human and you are vulnerable and you have all the feelings of a human heart. Acceptance. Most Christians would say, 'Yes, that is where you should come to. To accept the will of God.' And you know, I suddenly saw a parallel with the case of God taking us beyond forgiveness to love. It was not enough to forgive the person who did the wrong and leave it there. 'No,' God commanded. 'Go beyond forgiving to loving.' And in this case: *Go beyond acceptance to thanking God and rejoicing.*

You say, 'Wait a minute. That is unreasonable.'

I reply, unreasonable, perhaps, but not unspiritual.

In pondering my friend's case afterwards I was reminded of the apostle Paul and his thorn in the flesh. Paul was spiritually perceptive, exceedingly perceptive. In the matter of the thorn he opens a door and lets you look in at the beginning of an experience. You see him learning a spiritual truth, quickly appropriating it, and putting it to powerful effect. We do not know what that thorn was, although some of you may think you do. It may have been his eyesight (there were those who would have plucked out their own eyes to give to him). It may have been a speech impediment (it would appear that his speech was not regarded as being particularly impressive). It may have been a hundred and one things — and I reckon if it had been necessary for you to know what it was, Paul would have told you. Since he did not do this, let us leave it there!

You will find that with many spiritual people they will tell you so much of a matter, and no more. This is often quite intentional because, normally, spiritual people tell you what they think it's good for you to know, and not one bit more. Paul left it there. But here is the point: it was a thorn in the flesh. And a thorn can be a mighty sore thing. If it does not come out the pain normally gets worse, and the affected part can suppurate. You may have gone to sleep scarce knowing a thorn was there, but your blanket touches it and you know all about it by the time you waken up. You may not be able to get at it, and it causes you pain. Now everybody knows the kind of irritation this gives.

Paul's was a spiritual thorn, not just a physical thorn, and he could not get it out. It may, of course, have had a physical dimension, but it had got through to Paul's spirit. It had 'got to him', as we might say in modern parlance. It was so important that he asked to have it removed. And God did not do it.

Now there is a time to be persistent in prayer, like the importunate widow. And Paul had another go. But God did not agree. Paul still did not give up: he had another attempt about this thorn in the flesh. I imagine Paul's mind worked like this. 'This miserable thing is curtailing my usefulness.' If it was a stammering tongue, I can imagine his saying: 'How much better would I be able to preach if I had no impediment. How much better, how much more effective, how much more powerful would I be if I had no speech difficulty.'

Or if it was his eyesight which was affected, he might have said, 'You know I can only read for a few minutes at a time because of my eyes. O God, why am I in this condition? Why may I not see with normal vision and study and get to know Your Word more and more deeply? How much more effective a man would I be for You, Lord, if I could be rid of this thorn in the flesh!'

I imagine that there are many of my audience who

have your own secret disadvantages, your self-consciousness, your lack of confidence, your shyness, your inability to speak fluently — and oh, they will rise before you like a cloud. Have you not said in your heart, 'O God, if it wasn't for this, how much more I could do for You. If I didn't have this cross to carry, how much more could I achieve for You!' I imagine Paul said all of these things.

The Power of the Thorn

But God said, 'No.' He said, 'My grace is sufficient for you, and My strength is made perfect in weakness.' I imagine that from the moment that voice sounded, Paul took stock and began to understand. Just think about it. This thorn prevented him being dependent on his eloquence, if it was a voice problem; it prevented him from being self-sufficient in whichever area the trouble lay. It threw him on to God. That thorn pressed him on to the very heart of the Lord Jesus, and it brought a depth of relationship and a closeness of walk with Jesus that would not, I believe, otherwise have been there. I believe that as a result of that thorn, the power of God in his life increased, and the emanation of God to others deepened. That thorn nailed him in a peculiar way to the cross of Jesus. That spike, that thorn went through his very spirit, and nailed him to the cross. And here is where his perception becomes evident.

Onward to Rejoicing

The moment he saw the truth of it, he could say, 'Ah, Lord, thank you! Now I rejoice in my thorn, I rejoice that Your strength is made perfect in weakness. Then,

Lord, I choose to be weak in this sense, that You might be glorified and Your strength manifest.'

So we come to the case of my friend, mentioned earlier, who had accepted the will of God. He was then taken on to the next stage: to rejoice in the will of God, and to thank God actually and totally from a full heart: 'Thank You, Lord, that these circumstances came into my life, because I know You and I know that they were not accidental. Help me to put them to good use, that they may press me into the deeps of the heart of Christ. Then I will bless You, and I will kiss the cross that killed me, that I might come into fullness of life in Jesus Christ.'

Friends, in revival God does not merely deal with the rough side of sin. He deals with the finer points of sanctification, and He will not be satisfied with your mere acceptance of your cross. He will take you to a place where you will rejoice in His will, whatever that will may be, until you fade out and God becomes all in all. Blessed be the name of the Lord.

Invitation

Some of you have crosses that you have accepted and are carrying for Jesus' sake, hurts that you have taken to Him and that are under the blood, but still have the power to rankle and pain you if you revert to the natural. You have learned to live with them and to carry your crosses.[1] Are you prepared to go upward to the next step, to thank God and to rejoice in the thorn, in the pain, in the cross — or rather to rejoice as you realize the effect of these in driving you into the deeps of God? Go in joy, carry the cross with joy and in this you will glorify God. How many will choose this high plane of sanctification?

Note

[1] I speak here of crosses that are in the will of God — not matters from which God would give deliverance.

6 | SPIRITUAL WARFARE: 1

Over recent decades there has been an increasing awareness amongst Christians that there is a realm of spiritual warfare, and there has also been an increasing interest in the activity of Satan and his intervention in the world of men.

Further back in modern times there was a fairly general acceptance amongst evangelicals that Satan was one of the greatest of created beings who in his pride would have exalted his throne as high as the throne of God. He rebelled and was cast out of Heaven with his followers and has thereafter maintained undying enmity against God. He was seen as the Prince of this world, which was regarded as being in his hand. His part in the fall of man and his continued temptation of man through the centuries was recognized. His contest with Christ in the wilderness and subsequent actions leading to Calvary were all generally familiar, and Paul's teaching that *our wrestling is not against flesh and blood, but against the principalities, against the powers, against the world-rulers of this darkness, against the spiritual hosts of wickedness in the heavenly places* (Eph 6:12), were all part of the general pool of knowledge.

A Deepening Awareness

In more recent times, however, there has come, at least in some circles, a closer look at the functioning of Satan's kingdom and at the whole idea of spiritual warfare. The fact of demon activity was clearly seen as Christ ministered, and indeed many of the Gospel stories are related to Christ's casting demons out of individuals. He taught that the 'strong man' should be bound before the destruction of his goods.

The story of Daniel's experience of fasting and praying for three weeks before God's messenger got through to him seemed almost to be rediscovered and the struggle between Michael and the prince of the kingdom of Persia seemed to be peculiarly significant.

With the dawning of first the Pentecostal and then the Charismatic eras, interest in these matters quickened. Anointed preachers have come into very direct conflict with the powers of darkness and have known their enemy. This can be seen, for example, in the life of Smith Wigglesworth, an early pioneer.

I look back to my own perception of these matters over much of the century, and recollect that I had a general knowledge of what I have indicated above for most of that time, but have experienced a deepening involvement in spiritual conflict with the kingdom of Satan in more recent times.

Blumhardt, Lewis, Warner and Peretti

For myself and others Blumhardt's experiences as described in his book *Blumhardt's Battle* opened a window into the realm of spiritual warfare in a very special way.[1] The writings of C. S. Lewis, notably his *Screwtape Letters*, affected a very wide circle. These brought the realm of temptation and Satan and his emissaries' part in it very much to the surface. Lewis's unusual way of looking at the matter from the tempter's point of view was particularly effective.

More recently the conflict between Michael and the prince of the kingdom of Persia has been brought to the attention of the Christian public by various teachers. Warner's *Territorial Spirits* has focused attention on the whole subject of spiritual warfare. Also very recently the bestselling novels by Frank Peretti (*This Present Darkness*, *Piercing the Darkness* and *The Prophet*) have highlighted the ongoing conflict between Satan and God, darkness and light, demons and angels. The picture may not be particularly accurate in its details, but it is powerfully suggestive and has caught widespread attention.

Personal Beliefs

I should perhaps state some of my own beliefs before introducing readers to the following chapters. I believe in a real devil and in an army of demon entities who are active in our world, evilly influencing men. I believe in a wicked hierarchy of rulers of darkness having particular territorial regions as their preserves — sometimes particular towns or countries. I believe in demon possession and in deliverance of people from demons by the power of God. I frequently see demons cast out.

I believe in a realm of deep conflict in spiritual places — battles fought out between great powers both beyond and through human channels. I believe all this, but I also believe that much of the realm of spiritual warfare is more mundane and very greatly overlooked by followers of Christ. Some of the teachings which follow are given to provide a corrective — but not to deny the more hidden and deeply spiritual realms of conflict. Much of that innerness is shrouded in mystery and may not be fully revealed this side of eternity. It is a realm about which we may speculate and perchance be left in ignorance because God is not minded to allow us fuller knowledge.[2] In our fascinated speculation, however, do not let us neglect areas of vital concern to our ongoing work for God — areas all around us which are, but may not immediately appear to be, our battlefields.

Why Does Satan Bother?

I want to digress for a moment and view the essential nature of the conflict. Have you ever noticed how persistent Satan can be? For me there is an abiding mystery: why does it matter so much to him to destroy a soul? Why is he so opposed to every movement Godward in a person? What does he get out of trying to hold in bondage every single individual in a teeming world? I do not know. I suppose it may be because it is the nature of essential evil to do evil endlessly.

I must also say I face another mystery. I have always looked with wonder at the persistence of the love of God in Christ for the well-being of our every soul. Every little detail seems to matter to Him. Why is it so important to the Creator of the universe that one solitary soul, such as Peter, should love Him? We are as the very small dust of the balance, yet He loves us — loves us every one.

Shouldering Our Responsibility

On this occasion I have one thing in particular to speak about. Not now commitment; not now deliverance from evil power in particular, but something rather interesting that may prove helpful to some of you. There is one lady present who may be embarrassed just a little, but something she said after the August camp I have remembered very, very clearly. She spoke of the wonderful pleasure and joy she had in Christ in the July camp. Hers was a cloudless sky; it was glory all the way — until there came a point part way through the week where she felt God spoke to her and asked if she would now become a burden-bearer (I can't remember the exact words), and instead of being merely a sharer of blessing, become a carrier of responsibility and burden.

She said yes, and immediately she entered into conflict. She doesn't know this, but I noticed that she was having a very hard time. Faces tend to reflect experience. I felt she was really suffering. I did not talk to her then; indeed, I hardly said a word to her till very near the end of the week, when I spoke very briefly. What I am about to say now is not something that we have discussed. But this particular case has caused me to think of opening up a subject that I am not sure I ever have opened up before. It could be useful to the person concerned, and also to many others of you who have entered that same field, or who in God's time will enter it.

What Is Spiritual Warfare?

We speak of spiritual warfare, of battling with the hosts of darkness. Usually the language is 'away up there', and as people listen they get varying ideas as to what the words mean. I suppose in the minds of many there is the thought of dark forces, of struggling in an unseen world with evil powers, in line with the words, *For our wrestling is not against flesh and blood, but against the principalities, against the powers, against the world-rulers of this darkness, against the spiritual hosts of wickedness in the heavenly places* (Eph 6:12). We may get the picture of a remote world in which this kind of conflict is going on, and although our perception of the matter may be very dim, we think we should be in there fighting.

The truth is that the battle is often not like that at all, and the ideas that many people have of the battle, I suggest, are almost entirely erroneous. It really is not like that! Let me explain what it is like. Some of our company who are most used in the ministry of deliverance have mentioned at various times that there comes over them a feeling of heaviness as they encounter or are about to encounter Satan (I sometimes use that horrible modern slang word *yuckiness*). I may waken up in the morning and feel, 'M'mmm. There is something evil moving.' I may sense it in my spirit. I remember one morning when I wakened up I suddenly saw a demon. It had been very close to my head, but by the time I discerned it, it was going out the door, or rather the end of the room, through a wall. Having caught a sight of it, I understood the feeling of darkness on and around my spirit. I became very careful, wondering where difficulty would arise, where a probable assault would come, how it would come: I became aware of danger — not of danger away up there in the heavenlies but danger right down here on the earth and around my very feet.

Down to Earth

Take the point. You have this feeling that all is not well. There is a sense of trouble on the face of the waters, and you are not quite sure how it will come.

Now here is what may be a surprise to some of you. It is not necessarily a sensational matter, nor is it something vague, strange and remote. I will tell you how I often find it. Satan will look for a vulnerable point. We all have our vulnerable points, and they are different. There are things that will annoy and irritate you and on which you can be very easily jolted. There are things that touch me that might not touch you at all. I find again and again that when Satan assaults, it does not appear to be a satanic assault at all: nothing to do with Satan, in its first impact. Somebody has really upset you, and your peace is destroyed. Your reaction gets right out of proportion. It can be a disagreement with someone to whom you are very close. You may be hurt. It can be that somebody has done something that you feel is quite unjust, and it has angered you. All that is needed is that you be shaken out of your peace with Christ, to let the devil come in.

At this point most people think they are fighting a fight at a human level with their own carnality or somebody else's carnality, and it has nothing to do with spiritual warfare. My friend, this *is* spiritual warfare. This is how your enemy does it. It is not remote, far out on an abstract plane where it is not touching you personally. Satan comes in and he gets a hold of something that does touch you personally. It touches you deeply, and you are rocked on it. It can be a variety of things. It can be a sudden feeling of deep pain, and it can be quite irrational and out of proportion. It can be a fierce barb of jealousy. It can be a sudden memory of an earlier failure and a feeling of regret with a conviction that things can never be the same again and that you may as well give up the fight. Whatever the issue, it can trouble so much that you lose your peace with God, and you can't concentrate on spiritual things because the issue is so upsetting you.

It is often at a very natural level that the incursion comes. And it is there that you have to die to self. I have noticed that the devil is not only a liar; he is a fearful liar. You may just be about to be used in your ministry, and he will make a suggestion and build a picture in your deep mind. A subtle and quite believable lie is suggested, and you think, 'Well, that's possible. I wonder if that's true? And if it is true, then such-and-such and such-and-such all logically follow.' You become so upset that you feel you can't go on with what God has given you to do. There, my friend, you are in the very midst of spiritual warfare. You are wrestling against hell, although it may seem to you to be just a natural upset that's bothering you. Mark that the devil comes in on the wing of natural things.

I remember my own prolonged battle with Satan in this area. Before preaching I was regularly attacked. A problem would present itself just before I was due to begin: it had to be settled then: it was imperative. If I went that way I could dismally fail in giving the message. If I resisted the devil I could go on to victory. At first I deplored the attacks and the accuracy of the timing. At last I welcomed them, having noticed that they almost always came when something important was at stake and, if resisted, they resulted in victory. I don't mean I ever became happy at the coming of Satan. His presence is always hideous — but I knew that if he was there and I went through with God, I could expect a wonderful outcome.

A Particular Attack

Those of you who were at camp will remember the morning I had obvious trouble with my voice. What happened was very simple. At the physical level, there was a little phlegm, which was not abnormal; I tried to clear it, and didn't at first quite succeed. I made the mistake of raising my voice, and if you do that you can strain a vocal cord — the throat doesn't clear; you are in real trouble then. Those of you who were there may have noticed the fearful battle that ensued to get to a position where I could preach at all that morning. I think many of you recognized that Satan was probably in it: he did not want the delivery of that word. But what you don't realize is that immediately before that, I had been in an intense conflict with hell for most of an hour. You can actually get to the point where you recognize hell is after you and that Satan is deliberately trying to trip you and upset you with something that may have very little basis in reality at all. In the sharpness of the circumstances of a camp, that kind of thing can happen very readily. It was only by the grace of God that I got through that morning, but God had the ultimate victory, as you will recall.

Closer Detail

I don't think I am saying too much by saying this. I have often noticed that before a Saturday night or some other critical meeting, I may make a bantering remark that touches my daughter Mary on a raw nerve. She for her part may raise something that annoys me, just before we leave for the meeting. Often the things that cause the trouble are of little significance, but their timing is critical.

As you know, we are very good friends and we work

closely together, and for this kind of thing to happen is ridiculous. We have both learned to watch very, very carefully. If we neglect this, Satan can get in on incredibly small matters. That is how a good deal of spiritual warfare arises. It is not in a high and lofty realm where you are not caring and are not really deeply involved personally. It is at levels at which you can be deeply irritated and suffer personally.

As I look around, I know so many of you, and I know how things work with you. In the case of one person who is present, she can be shaken again and again unnecessarily. Often the things which trouble her provide a real appearance of justification. But there is never justification for allowing anything to break the tie between you and God.

And so for those of you who are coming into the beginning of spiritual warfare, you will find that Satan will attack you; he will look for your vulnerable parts. You may be of an introspective turn of mind. I was, and he put me through hell because of my introspection. I didn't realize I was fighting with the devil. I thought, 'That's just how I am made, and I suffer from this.' Satan was using that part of my make-up, my temperament, to bind me and to prevent me coming into the ministries that God wanted to use me in. It will help if you can understand what is actually happening. It is not just that you are having a battle with something in you: Satan is using that area for carrying his battle into the core of your life. You have to take your areas of vulnerability to God. You have to say, 'O God, even if I don't understand and even if my feelings are hurt, Christ is Lord.'

And, you know, on the morning earlier referred to, God broke the power of Satan in my first battle with him in a moment of time, and I was through to God, and I was fine — and then my voice broke. Of all the dirty tricks, when you have had a mighty battle and you have ultimately got the victory, he comes in with a side thrust — you have the material to preach but no voice with which to do it! This is an exceedingly frustrating situation. We don't talk much about hatred in Christian circles; but I hate the devil. And I tell you, when I find him on the run, there is no mercy of Christ comes through me where Satan is concerned. He is cruel; he is a destroyer, he is a killer. When the heel of Christ is on his head, I rejoice with exceeding great joy.

No Surrender

Now there is one other thing I want to say. Never give in. Never surrender. I had great respect for one of you who was preaching on the morning that the elements almost drowned her out and we weren't sure if the marquee would be blown away. She fought it through right to the end, and the blessing of God was there. Now I want all of you to develop that characteristic. Never give in. If I had sat down because my throat was a bit shaggy, I would have felt defeated; I would have felt horrible; I couldn't have stood it. I don't know what I would have done if my voice had gone altogether. But I did not believe God would allow that to happen. God makes you trust Him in dire circumstances when there seems no way through.

I believe in miracle that occurs in the actual moment of need. Those of us who are deeply involved in ministry are seeing more and more miracle. Where you are at the end of your tether and you can do nothing, the living God steps in and He works His own miracle. Those of you who have been tricked by Satan, who have been in conflict and haven't recognized it as part of your warfare but thought that it was just part of yourself, forget it. If you have come to God, to put your life at His disposal, to allow Him to fight His battle through you, you will find that you are often fighting that battle but not recognizing it for what it is. That *is* the battle.

> PROPHECY: *The Lord sees you, what you are and who you are, and He knows you altogether, what you are. And a bright light has shone out of Heaven, and it has shone upon the pinnacle of the mountain I have called you to climb, and it shines down upon you, the climber, as you stretch yourself to reach the pinnacle, as you stretch the very body's capacities, and there is within you a striving for that place of vision that has been shown to your life, and that vision is clear as the top of the mountain, and it is clear to you as your eyes are trained upon the top of the mountain, and as there is a steadfast following after that light that shines upon the pinnacle. And all joy is yours as you come up out of the fog, and in the first moment as your faith breaks through the fog into that clearer air there is a joy in your being. When you have been faithful in the time of fog, the light finds you with your face upward, and a steadfast hope within you. And if it be, my child, that in the climb through fog you lost your way, you lost your bearings, and you lost your hope, and your head was down, then when the light shines, when the fog has lifted and you are out into the clearer air, it may take a little time before your soul is aware of the change in the atmosphere, the change in the spiritual currents. But if you lift your face towards the pinnacle of the mountain again, quickly the rays of light shall shine upon your face, and swiftly the healing warmth shall enter into your body and into your spirit, and chords you thought were broken will vibrate again, and areas within your being that you felt were deadened by the force of the conflict shall*

*come alive again, and joy which seemed a thing of
the past shall again spill over as with the joy of
childhood, as with the carefree, brimming laughter
of an infant: so shall it rise again, the song of the
lips and the song of the heart, and the praises of the
Most High crowd together in heart and body, spirit,
soul and mind, to give forth to the glory of your
God. Shout for joy, all ye saints, shout aloud for
joy, all you that love Zion. Shout for joy, for there is
a King, and your Redeemer is strong. Though you
are weak, shout for joy, for your Redeemer is strong
in the midst of you. Oh, happy are the people who
do know their God. Carefree is the spirit which
walks in the aloneness of the high places with the
Lord, the God of Israel. Be confident of this one
thing, that when the life is stretched to the utmost,
there am I in the midst of you.*

Note

1 Johann Christoph Blumhardt was an eminent German minister of the nineteenth century. His official report of his
experiences has been translated by Frank S. Boshold in
Blumhardt's Battle: A Conflict with Satan (Thomas E.
Lowe, 1970).

2 Since writing this section the subject of spiritual warfare
has been increasingly before me and may be the subject of a
later book. This will touch aspects not covered here.

7 | SPIRITUAL WARFARE: 2

The following testimony is to a healing that occurred immediately after my first address on spiritual warfare. Because it is relevant also to what comes after, the testimony is included here.

Morag

SEVERE PAIN: I am going to speak about two things that seem unrelated but were in fact very closely related.

I hadn't been well for about three weeks. When the trouble started, I thought I had flu. I couldn't stop shaking and shivering, and my muscles and bones were sore — everything was sore. I didn't bother at first. As most of you know, I have my own business, so that I can't just go home when I feel like it. But one day things got really bad, and I had to go home. I could not drive on; I didn't have a single bit of energy. If I was going upstairs I'd have to stop halfway to rest; I felt as though my muscles were seizing up. The tiredness was so great that I thought that some disease or illness was creeping up on me. I went to the doctor eventually (prompted by my mum — you know what mothers are like!). He diagnosed exhaustion, and told me I was heading for a breakdown. The only way I could get out of his office was to tell him, 'Right, I'll go home and

rest.' But I didn't rest, and there was no improvement.
Mr Black prayed for me, and there was just nothing. I
know what it is to be instantly healed, I know the glory
of it. But this time there was nothing.

HATRED: While all this was going on, something else
was happening — and I didn't think the two matters
were connected until I heard last week's sermon.* It
was last week (while I was still unwell) that one of my
husband's sisters was married. My husband James is
the oldest brother in the family; his father is dead. I
thought that it was James's place to walk his sister
down the aisle. But I was seemingly the only one who
thought that, and it was his younger brother who gave
her away. I didn't realize it, but this was eating at me. It
got so bad (I think because I was really ill as well) that I
couldn't speak to the family. If they came into our
shop, I felt ill. If I saw them, I would go into the back of
the shop. But I still thought this was just because I
wasn't well. I didn't think anything else.

As time went on, however, since I wasn't getting any
better I thought, 'This is more than a physical or even a
mental illness.' I knew in my heart there was something else. But I didn't know what it was, until I came
on my own to the meeting on Saturday. James had gone
to his sister's wedding, meaning to come on to church
afterwards — which he did, about nine o'clock — but he
couldn't get in, not knowing to press a switch that
would attract attention. I was sitting up at the back
impatiently waiting. James had said he would be in
shortly after seven o'clock, but he hadn't come. On top
of this feeling of illness and the bad feeling I had
towards his family, I began to think, 'He's drinking.'

---

* See preceding chapter.

Now James had had a drink problem earlier, and although he had been wonderfully delivered I thought, 'After that first toast, that will be him. He'll be drinking the rest of the night.'

So there I was sitting, a nervous wreck. I still didn't put two and two together, until Mr Black started his sermon. It was about satanic attacks, and how on a small matter we can let the devil in. And I realized that was what had happened to me. I had let hatred build up in my mind. I thought, 'How could anyone, how could I, hate someone, a family, the way I did?' It was true hatred that I had towards James's family, and that was why I wasn't getting better. That was why even when Mr Black had prayed for me, and when I had prayed myself and read my Bible, there was nothing. In entertaining this hatred, I had let the devil in. I am a person that he does attack, and I am very conscious of his attacks; I always have been.

FORGIVENESS AND HEALING: At about nine o'clock, realizing what had been happening to me, I thought, 'That's it. I'm definitely going to Mr Black for prayer.' In the instant that I thought that, our Lord took it away. I had been sitting exhausted, sore, even my back feeling crippled. And when I had realized my sin through the preaching (it was as though Mr Black was speaking directly to me), in a flash the Lord took it away, and I felt as though a knife had cut through ropes. I got up — physically, mentally, spiritually. It was absolutely marvellous. I haven't looked back since, and I don't now have any hatred towards my in-laws. What they do is up to them. I just don't have any resentment — it is truly amazing.[1]

And James wasn't drinking! At that same moment when the Lord released me from the devil, I knew that he hadn't been drinking. It must have been about the same time that he was trying to get into the church, and we didn't know!

The difference it has made to me I can't get over to people. I just know how I feel inside. When I tried to tell someone that evening about my release, I found it difficult to express what it meant and how I felt. But that night I opened my Bible at 1 Corinthians 2:

> *For I determined not to know anything among you, save Jesus Christ, and Him crucified. And I was with you in weakness, and in fear, and in much trembling* (1 Cor 2:2–3).

That completed it for me! And although I don't use fancy words, I hope that the glory of the Lord is coming through.

HB: This is an important testimony. It's ill business for us to be praying over one or other of you when you are really regarding iniquity in your heart, when you are not right with God, when there are things that are obviously wrong. God again and again goes to the heart of the matter, and it is wonderful. He shows in a moment of time what He requires. And the moment you meet His demand you can expect the miracle to happen. I do appreciate this testimony tonight. Thanks very much, Morag. And James — I'm sorry for you. I remember when £30 worth of alcohol was poured down the drain when God dealt with you a few years ago — and to think you were suspected!

> PRAYER: *We pray that there will be a full transmission of Your word. Lord, we feel the drawing near of the Holy Spirit, and we pray that nothing will be lost in what You would convey to men. We thank You for all Your kindness on other*

occasions: the manifestation of Christ, the
revelation of that lovely One. O Lord our God, we
pray that You will be glorified. We ask it in His
name and for His sake. Amen.

Understanding the Battle

You heard reference in this testimony to my previous
address on spiritual warfare, and it may be of interest to
you that I think I have had more comment on that
sermon than on any sermon for years. It may also interest you to know that had I been putting my sermons in
my order of priority over these years, last week's would
probably have come very near the bottom. It was very
brief. It was almost a part, I suppose, of a camp report,
following on from that occasion. I thought it was
exceedingly simple. And it has caused me to wonder. I
dare not in any way take away from the sermon, since I
felt God in it, but I have been surprised at the amount of
feedback that has come from it, and this has caused me
to think about it deeply, and to continue tonight with
the same subject, although treating it this time a little
differently.

Our warfare is not against flesh and blood, but
against principalities and powers, against spiritual
wickedness in heavenly places (Eph 6:12). *When the*
enemy shall come in like a flood, the Spirit of the Lord
shall lift up a standard against him (Is 59:19 AV). I
indicated last week that a great deal of the warfare is
not airy-fairy, fancy, high in the sky, in areas that don't
really interest you or trouble you; that the warfare
comes right to your doorstep. It comes right through the
door of your life into the things that surround you from
day to day.

Satan's Tactics

Let me remind you of a typical experience in my own life. I found that one of the recurring contexts of spiritual warfare was immediately before preaching. Again and again just before preaching I was assaulted. It wasn't a case of seeing a dark demon visually — but just at the critical time there would come to my memory something or other that troubled me, and it would rise up before me with the suggestion, 'You'll need to get this sorted. You'll need to get your mind clear about this.' I would begin to panic. I was due to preach, and there was this insistent demand: 'You'll never have liberty to preach if you don't get this business sorted out in your mind.' And I gradually began to realize that this was warfare: this was spiritual warfare. The devil was attacking my mind — until I came to a place with God where I used to say, 'I'm having nothing more to do with this; I'm not going to think about it; I'm not going to touch it. It's over there. I have one thing to do, which is to be the channel of the living God.' And as soon as the meeting was over and I thought back to the troubling thing, it was a little molehill of no great significance. But it had assumed gigantic proportions and it had been planted there to prevent God getting through.

You will find that the devil will look for your every area of vulnerability. You may be prone to jealousy, and if you are, at a critical time something will happen; somebody will say something; and it will stir the whole evil bed; the jealousy will rise like a giant before you, and you won't get through to God. It may be resentment. It may be, as with Morag, deep hatred. You may think you are dealing with bad relatives or bad situations, and the fact of the matter is that the devil is exploiting these things and using them to get in to break you and bind you and hold you under his grip. Many of you will have found that you never do get victory by battling with these things. The more you think about your hatred the worse it gets. The more you think about your resentment the worse it gets. The more you think about the injustices that have been done and perpetrated upon you, the worse they get. You try to fight it out, and you try to fight it out, and at the end of the day you are a quivering wreck, and unless God comes in to lift you, you are in total disarray.

The assaults can come in 'good' ways, so to speak. I remember not long after I was baptized in the Holy Spirit I was very interested in the writings of Charles G. Finney. There is a chapter in his lectures on revival that causes many people to be extremely introspective. I was naturally introspective, and the chapter made me much more so. I began to get increasingly bound as I worried over what to do about sins of omission and commission — I got bound to the extent that Miss Taylor almost gave me up, fearing that I would never make anything of spiritual life. God had to break that bondage. Satan can come in even on a good thing and push it too far and catch you.

Paul could say, *We are not ignorant of his devices.* Now I can't say that, because again and again he catches me with a new device. I do learn, and I don't always get caught twice the same way. Yet he has many, many weapons in his armoury. But I would get this through to you right at the beginning: do not associate spiritual warfare too exclusively with the more spectacular part of Peretti's scenario where angels and demons fight it out in the skies. His basic idea probably derives from that part of Scripture where Daniel is seen praying for twenty-one days before he gets victory. The battle was going on in the heavenlies. But that which was before Daniel, I imagine, would be very down to earth. He would have to be resolute in obeying the leading of God, and remain in a fasting condition and carry the burden that God had put upon him. That was spiritual warfare.

Now I am going to give you some examples. I like taking examples from ongoing events — particularly from very recent events. And I am going to illustrate the subject that way now.

How Should We Respond?

Recently a group of four of us were travelling a long distance by car. I was in the passenger seat when I began to feel spiritual forces coming down powerfully against me, strong forces. These were not related, so far as I knew, to any particular issue. Neither was it a mental assault. I knew there could possibly be one or two things in the background, but I wasn't quite sure that it was related to any of them. Now as it happens I seldom ask God questions. Many people do, but I don't tend to live that way. I do, however, open my spirit to receive His revelation. I look for an opening road, and it is enough for me if I have freedom to go that way. If God shuts a door, He shuts a door. I don't look into the future beyond what I feel He is wanting to reveal. On the occasion in the car I felt these forces coming and was not sure why, but I found that I was spiritually in what was like a cocoon. It was not safe for me to reach out in various directions, or think about a number of issues, or become involved in deep conversation. I found I was hemmed in with God. And it was as though hell was raging all around me. The others continued their own conversations or private reflections while I was in this place apart.

Now this should be of interest to you. How do you fight out a spiritual battle? Well, you don't. It is as simple as that: you don't. And if you try to, you will get into a fearful mess. I took the attitude, 'I am a child of God. I am a channel for the life of God. The battle is not mine, but the Lord's. I have nothing to do with this but to abide in Christ.' Gradually I felt the growth of power within me, of life within me. I didn't know what circumstances would unveil themselves, but I knew the Lord of circumstances, and I knew that in God I had the grip, that God was in control, and no device of evil would prosper. I asked no questions, but I got spiritual power to face the things that were lying immediately ahead. God intervenes miraculously in the affairs of men, and He intervened in the affairs of people who were in desperate need just at that time. I was reminded of recent preaching. You remember that when Laban would have taken Jacob and all his company back into his land and under his control, God appeared to Laban on the previous night and said, *Speak to my servant Jacob neither good nor ill.* In other words, 'Don't touch him! Keep your hand off!'

Jacob would be much encouraged. But in a very short time word came to him that his sworn enemy, his brother Esau, was coming to meet him with four hundred armed men, having sworn to have his life. Years before he had sworn it. Jacob was now in real trouble. He had manipulated and manoeuvred through much of a lifetime. He had been astute, and he had got his own way again and again. But see him now at the brook Jabbok. He is up against an impossible situation, and he knows he can manipulate nothing. But the angel of God came and wrestled the last of Jacob out of him, if I might put it that way. Jacob then was crippled, rendered unable to proceed in his own strength. He was made totally dependent on the living God.

And God altered the mind of Esau, so that he came in peace. Leave your battles with the Lord. Let the Lord carry the battle, and you will find He will change the hearts and lives of men and women, some of whom might be minded to do you harm. God changes people, He controls people. His hand that holds the universe can hold all the issues of your life.

Now, friends, that was spiritual warfare. In the personal case described above I could have gone down in a panicking flood. But God acted and moved. I did nothing but stand aside.

Let me remind you of the occasion when Miss Taylor expressed her bewilderment after a telephone call in which the action of God had been such that she did not know why she had been involved at all, for she felt she had done nothing. That, I told her, was why she was there. That is what God wants with people. He wants people who will get out of the way. He wants you to be in a position where He can move through you and fight the battle through you and overcome through you. But the human 'you' is out of the way. You don't join in the battle. He carries the battle through. Blessed be the name of the Lord.

Almost Incredible Evil

Recently I was in touch with my friend Drew Greenwood,[2] who spoke to me about the work of a lady whom God has been deeply using. I don't want to identify the person, for reasons which will become evident. Drew was very keen that I should meet her. My day had been particularly busy, and it was fairly late when I was able to contact her by phone and arrange for her to come with her husband from Glasgow to Greenock for a late meal.

Spiritual warfare...She is one of the most persecuted Christians, I reckon, in Britain today. She has been deeply involved in dealing with the consequences of child abuse, ritual abuse and satanic activity, and is in touch regarding these matters with members of parliament, assistant chief constables and Scotland Yard. There is, across the country, a flood of horror. I am not going in detail into that flood. The things that are done to children are unspeakable, and the murder groups who are active you can hardly conceive of in twentieth century Britain. With very little support, on a voluntary basis, she has become skilled in the work she does. She has been on television. There was a programme just recently which vilified her. Indeed, there has been a declaration, 'We must stop this woman. Her work is powerful and effective.' The dirty tricks that are played, you could scarcely believe — such as photographing her with a man while her husband was with them, but cutting the husband out of the photograph so that it can be printed with innuendo. Horrible lies are circulated about her.

She was in America for a particular conference, and there was a satanic plant in the group that was there. Almost immediately things were set rolling against her and a murder plan was devised to kill her. The pressures became intense, but ultimately the enemy realized that although they got to the point of almost assassinating her they were unable to carry this out because of the angelic protection around her. This is spiritual warfare. She is fighting for lives — young, damaged lives, older people who have done damage to lives and are themselves damaged. Spiritual warfare.

Spiritual Recognition

She related some very interesting things. For example, she said that when she meets a satanist, there is very quick reaction, because the demon(s) within the satanist will look for any vulnerable point within her. If people are involved in this kind of work, the satanist will know almost immediately where the weaknesses lie. If it is a weakness on the line of sex they pick it up to exploit it. If it is in the line of covetousness — whatever the weakness is within the person — the demons will recognize it and play on it. Immediately the person concerned will find himself or herself in spiritual warfare with the demon powers.

Spiritual recognition works in other ways too. Within seconds of seeing this lady, I spontaneously assessed her as a very good person, a kindly, warm person; but very quickly I realized she was iron-strong: there was that combination.

I want to mention something that Jimmy Lunan was telling me very recently.[3]

Jimmy, as you know, had a wonderful deliverance some little time ago. Although he had been saved and baptized in the Spirit and healed from rheumatoid arthritis and a fractured ankle, both in a moment of time, there was still a demon (or demons) to be dealt with. With his wife Maureen he had seen a vision of angels, but he still had a demon. He had been a protestant gang leader (though he married a Catholic, with all the family consequences that that brought), and as such had a very violent background. God's hour to deal with him had at last come. There was real violence in Jimmy from early days. He knew the truth about himself, and one of our leaders, Grace Gault, discerned his condition and prayed with him. Quickly it became apparent that the demon grip was extremely strong and others were called in to control his reactions. He was a gentleman and did not want to hurt anybody, but knew what the demons might do through him.

He was completely delivered, but he tells me that before the deepest, darkest, most violent demon came out, suddenly it was as though he was looking on events from the side, and he saw what the demon was doing. Evidently it was looking round the praying company (about six of us) to see if there was anyone without a covering, anyone whom it could attack or enter. I imagine that there would have been real violence, had there been such an opening — that Jimmy would have been driven, actually driven, to be violent at that point. But there was none there uncovered. Jimmy indicated that we were not equally covered. But, thank God, we were all covered.

The Area of Conflict

Spiritual warfare. Let me reiterate what I have said earlier. We fight not against flesh and blood, but against principalities and powers, spiritual wickedness in high and in heavenly places. And we don't just fight them '*up there*': we fight them *down here, in here, in the heart, in the mind, and in the will*. These are the real areas of conflict. That is where much of the battle rages. So often you think, 'Oh, such-and-such is my weakness. I am born this way.' Yes, that may be so. But the devil exploits that weakness and comes in on it. You think you are merely fighting a human condition, when in fact you are in conflict with evil power exploiting a human condition. And that, my friend, is spiritual warfare.

One of you phoned me at about three o'clock this morning, having wakened from a fearsome nightmare with the feeling that the house was deeply affected, and with a raging headache — desperate for the touch of God. Now I believe the devil has been really after that life — and yet in a moment of time there came the hand of God and His peace.

I want you to know that you are altogether known of God, and you are also uncomfortably known by demon powers. Life is not a safe place for the careless. You need to walk with God. What manner of men then ought we to be in all holy manner of living and godliness? Search your heart.

Areas of Danger

I remember Johnny Anderson. One or two of the older folks here may remember him too. There was nobody quite like Johnny Anderson. He had a very unusual voice, and his preaching was quite unique. He was one of those who was early used in deliverance ministry, when there was very little of it in the country. I remember his telling of one occasion where a lady came forward in one of his meetings — I don't know whether she was going to attack him or exactly why she had come, but I think she collapsed at his feet. As she lay prostrate he looked at his watch and said, 'In two minutes from now, this demon is coming out. Where will it go? What kind of life are you living? How safe are you?' There was consternation. One minister, I gather, was found hanging on to the pulpit rails in considerable fear. If you were present in a company where demons were being driven out, how safe would you be? Where would they go? How clean are you? How real are you? How deeply are you in touch with God?

Secure Ground

Oh, I feel the love of Christ now. He loves you with an everlasting love. He has not come to terrify you; He has come to set you free. Blessed be His name. He has come to bind the strong man and to destroy his goods, to take his every effect out of your every life, to set you free into the glorious liberty of the sons and daughters of God. He is the Lamb of God. They crucified Him at Calvary. They thought they would kill the Son of God. I wonder if they forgot God the Son. The Son of God rose again and there never had been any possibility of killing God the Son. He arose in triumph with healing in His wings. He paid the price on Calvary that makes it possible for you and me to be set totally free from our every affliction, physical and spiritual. He came that we might have life and that we might have it abundantly. The price of our freedom was paid on Calvary's tree. You came there for salvation. Why now carry needless burdens, when He has borne them to the tree? Come that you might have life. Remember the Isaiah scripture that Christ quoted at the outset of His ministry: *The Spirit of the Lord is upon me, because he anointed me to preach good tidings to the poor: he hath sent me to proclaim release to the captives, and recovering of sight to the blind, to set at liberty them that are bruised* (Luke 4:18). The healing of wounds, the freeing of the prisoners. Life, abundant life.

What about that dark one? Ah, you are afraid of the dark one out there and what he will do. Speaking carefully, I am not now afraid of the dark one. I will tell you why I am not afraid of him. It is because I know the Holy One. I can now better understand Smith Wigglesworth and Miss Taylor, who had similar experiences — who knew the attention of Satan so persistently, so constantly, that in Miss Taylor's case when she wakened on one occasion to find the devil sitting at the end of her bed (she would actually see him visually), she looked at him and said, 'Och, it's just you again' — and turned over and went to sleep.

I have seen demons on two occasions; they are horrible. They leave a 'yucky' feeling behind them. Worse than 'yucky' — horrific. What do you do? Concentrate on them and how terrible they are? Not at all. It is light that drives out darkness. You concentrate on Christ. He deals with all the demon power and the darkness. Don't turn toward darkness. Turn toward light, and live in the light. He will give you power over all the power of the enemy, and you will cease to fear the devil. Fear is one of the weapons with which he binds men. Never fear the devil. Fear God, but never fear the devil. When you walk with God, you may know the reality of having power over all the power of the enemy.

I am actually thrilled with what happened to me in the car on the occasion earlier mentioned. I did nothing, nothing, but just kept in the presence of God, and let the battle go raging through me till I knew I had the grip in God for whatever circumstance life might bring. God is on the throne, God is in control.

If you are conscious that the devil has a grip on certain areas or is troubling on certain points, come to Christ to find His fullness, His victory, His overcoming power. Come and you will be received.

> PRAYER: *You know our every circumstance. You know the areas that that dark one would darken and bind. You know, Lord, Your power to set men free.... The moment we have faith, the miracle can take place. Lord, we believe in You. We believe in Your power and in Your willingness to set free the sons of men. Lord, we pray that all who come shall know, perchance without personal ministry, the liberating power of the living God.*

Continue Your work now as people respond. Let the anointing be powerful, we pray You. Let there be a setting free of men and women into the glorious liberty of the sons of God. We ask it in Christ's name and for His sake. Amen.

Notes

[1] Morag was further amazed when, just as this book was going to print over a year later, the brother-in-law who had acted as best man at his sister's wedding said to her one day, 'You know, Morag, you are an inspiration to us all!'

[2] Drew Greenwood is known to many as a leader in the Full Gospel Business Men's Fellowship.

[3] For the story of Jimmy Lunan's healing from rheumatoid arthritis and the vision of angels he shared with his wife Maureen, see my book *Christ the Deliverer* (New Dawn Books, 1991), chap. 9 and Appendix 3.

8 | THEY WERE IN THE WARS

In this chapter I bring you contributions from three others — Grace, Diana and Kathleen — which were first given to listening audiences. The first two deal very directly with aspects of spiritual warfare and the third with internal strife, in which of course Satan was greatly interested.

Grace

CONFLICT BEFORE VICTORY: I found that before going to our annual August camp this year the conflict was very, very severe. It frequently is so before a camp, and especially before the August camp. I knew from the type of conflict that there would be need of deliverance ministry, and that Satan was really minded to oppose the work of God on many fronts. I usually find, in fact I think I have always found, that when there is a particular level of conflict, there is also a similar level of victory and there are positive results. There is a part of me which almost dreads the conflict until the results come, but when the victory comes I tend to forget the earlier battle.

There has been one line of ministry that God has been bringing more and more before me, and I have come to the conclusion that at least some of the recent conflict was aimed at preventing this ministry from operating or being spoken about.

HEALING THE HIDDEN WOUNDS: This ministry relates to situations where there has come deep hurt into life, leaving scars that only Christ can heal. It came very sharply to my attention just how deep can be the unhealed areas, when one night someone came to speak to me, initially on an unrelated topic. As we were speaking, the presence of God deepened in the room, and they suddenly began to open up something that was very private and painful. They began to weep before God until there came a healing. It made me realize how very deep can be the hurts and the scars carried even by deep Christians.

I subsequently spoke publicly along that line and discovered immediately that there was a strong response, and God began to move. You will appreciate that it is very difficult to speak in any detail about this, because the things revealed are so private that I may not go anywhere near identifying them. But there is a verse that has been living for me: *If there be any consolation in Christ, any comfort of love...* There are times when you feel you could weep yourself as people reveal deep hurts that they have carried all their lives in total privacy, but it is wonderful when they suddenly realize that Christ loves them and they can tell their hurts to Him. It just needs the pouring in of the love of Christ to bring healing. As they are taken back into the situation where the hurt first arose, they find Christ comes and stands with them. It is as though He goes back into the past and is there in that situation, and there comes the healing of His love. Very often along with the hurt there has been left a terrible anger and resentment against the one or ones who inflicted the hurt.

THE PROBING OF THE SPIRIT: I will give one instance, because the person concerned has testified to this. One lady felt a blockage where her baptism in the Spirit was concerned. She was baptized, but it was as though she was only just inside the door. As she was prayed with, it became very evident that she carried a lot of hurt, although she herself had no idea of it until the Spirit probed. It is not a case of sitting down and thinking out what could be causing a blockage or whether there are any unhealed wounds in the past. In this lady's case it was simply that as she was being prayed with, the Spirit Himself showed her an incident away back in early childhood. It had caused terrible pain. She had carried it all her life and never told a soul. It had created a blockage, and in her case there was need for actual deliverance. It is a wonderful thing that Christ can come in in a moment. But sometimes it doesn't happen in a moment; sometimes the healing of these inner hurts can take a longer time. But for this person it did happen very quickly. Christ's healing and His love came in, the past was healed, and the wound was healed. Sometimes it is more of an ongoing process. I think that a lot can depend on how much a person is being faithful to Christ, how much they are wanting Him. Where there is a deep desire for Him, He is able to meet at the very deepest levels of need. Remember the hymn:

> Such love, pure as the whitest snow,
> Such love weeps for the shame I know,
> Such love...

There is no limit to what that love can do. *If there be any consolation in Christ, any comfort of love...*I have a total confidence (I would die for this truth) that there is no hurt that Christ cannot heal. The very depth of the deepest valley that we can go into, His light can reach, and it brings healing and comfort and makes a life new. Blessed be His name.

Mr Black's Comments

For some time the preparation of a company for deliverance ministry was largely left to me. Under God I seemed to be able to stir troubling entities and bring people to a sense of need and to a place where they positively sought to be free. More recently I have become aware that Grace fulfils the same function but in a different way. Her ministry touches deep chords, and the compassion of Christ draws people as with a magnet. In the circumstances I am now including more detail about this area from some of her earlier speaking, which provides further insights.

Grace: The Pearl

GUARDED FROM CHILDHOOD: Having found Christ as Saviour at an early age, I grew up with an inner knowledge of certain protective barriers that should not be crossed. I think probably everyone, Christian and non-Christian, has these. And one of the things that I sensed should never be done was to allow a hardness to come into my spirit. I sensed that one's spirit should be towards God like a flower that opens up to the sun, and that the warmth of the Son of God, the sun of righteousness, coming on a life would enable this to happen.

I was very early aware that there should be that openness where God was concerned. And I felt very distinct warnings at various times in my life, when situations had arisen that were extremely hurtful and difficult to live with — some of them when I was quite young. I remember being terribly tempted to let a hardness grow round me, to take a course of action that would have brought a hardness towards certain people. But I knew in my spirit, without any doubt at all and without speaking to anybody about it, that it would also bring a hardness towards God. Something in me that was wide open to God would close, and I would not know Christ in the same way as I did and as I wanted to. And so I was never allowed to let that hardness in.

HURTS BRINGING HARDNESS: I have become aware in recent years in particular, sometimes in speaking to people or praying with them, that such a hardness has come in — often to lives that have not known Christ at an early age, or have not known Him deeply. Some have had very difficult pasts, with very deep hurts. These they have covered and never spoken about to anybody. I think that this line of teaching is most applicable to lives who are in earnest about going on with God and are really hungry for Him. Again and again I have noticed that they could get so far through to God, but then would come up against a barrier. In some cases there could be a demon involved, but very often it was not so. I would often observe that even where there was no demonic barrier, there was a very real barrier that just could not be passed. A life would get so far with God, but the hunger would not be met: the person would not get right through.

Let me give an illustration which may make the matter understandable. When an oyster is irritated by a grain of sand under its shell, it emits a protective fluid which solidifies to form a pearl. Now a pearl looks lovely, but it is very hard. The oyster grows that hardness around the pain, and that is exactly what many people do — I think particularly people who are quite strong and able in many ways to cope. They grow a defensive shell, a defensive hardness, around their spirits.

There is a better way. Instead of developing that defence and shrugging the hurt off or burying it as though it hadn't happened, so that it just lodges inside, we bring it to Christ. We bring to Him every hurt as it comes into life (and it comes into every life). In the moment that it is received we bring it to Christ. As we do so, it may briefly seem to get worse. We suddenly feel the full intensity of the pain. But as we receive it and then give it to Christ, the poison of it, the unbearable part, just drains out, and we are left with His sweetness and His healing. There comes in us a tenderness towards Christ and an openness to Him.

BREAKING THE SHELL: When I spoke about this in one of our meetings and gave advice as to how to deal with hurt, a number of people came to me afterwards. One of them who spoke to me some time later said she had put the teaching into practice with wonderful effect. But then as she had gone on putting it into practice, it hadn't been quite so wonderful. She had discovered that there were areas of deep hurt inside that she thought she had learned to cope with but that she now realized had just been buried too deep. This was a person who was very keen for God. I had sensed again and again when I was with her that she would get so far, but couldn't get right through to having her inner heart hunger met. And I knew as she spoke to me what the problem was. I advised her to open it all up to Christ, just to tell it to Him as she was telling it to me, and really let Him in — let Him come into all the situations of the past. She did so as much as she could and got quite a lot of help that night. But full healing does not always happen instantly, and over the weeks that followed she continued to try to open herself up more and more to Christ, until she came to a crisis point.

I would emphasize this: she was desperate for God, desperately hungry for God Himself. She was aware that it might not be too serious to have defences in place with human beings. To let people get to know us and come into our lives at a certain level, but not beyond that, is one thing. But to transfer that attitude to God is another. Yet many do it, only letting Him into a certain part and not beyond.

INCOMING OF LOVE: That night she absolutely opened up. I suppose she was so hungry for God that something burst inside, and she opened up the deep, deep part in her that had been so terribly hurt, and she let Christ touch it. He took her back to the very first time that level of pain had come into her life. I don't know whether she had actually forgotten the first time until that moment, but she was taken right back to it; and Christ was there.

I sensed that with this person it was important that she should really forgive the one responsible for the hurt. I felt it hard actually to say this to her, because I myself would not have found it easy to forgive; I don't think anyone would. It took a miracle. Without hesitation she said, 'Oh, yes!' And in the instant that she did so, she was flooded with love — love for that other, but above all, love for Christ. The love of Christ flooded through her like a sunburst. I had an awareness too of calling and anointing and of spiritual life being wide open to her. The love of God was shed abroad in her heart. As she put it, she found a love she didn't know existed anywhere. She found it in the Lord Jesus Christ.

It is only in Christ that we find love in completeness. It is only there that we find it in fullness. It is only there that we find full, complete healing, no matter how deep the wound has been. He is the Healer, He is the completion, and you can safely trust that deep part of your being to Him, because He will never hurt it, He will never deceive you. He will never even inadvertently hurt that part of you. Someone you love might accidentally hurt you in that deep part. Sometimes someone you love knows that they do it; they cheat on you. But Christ never, never does. You can trust Him.

I am struck sometimes by the number of people who will come to one or other of us at home or away, some of them quite well on in life, who as they have responded to this kind of teaching have said, 'You know, I have never told anybody this. I never thought I would be able to speak about it.' They suddenly find that they are able to open it up to Christ. The human to whom they are speaking is only an intermediary; it is actually God to whom they are opening up, and as they open up, He heals. It might hurt for a little as a wound is probed. But it is only for a moment, and it is as nothing compared with the beauty, the joy, and the love that Christ gives in exchange.

Christ wants to give that love to each one of us. He wants to pour in and pour in, until we are like flowers that are wide open in the sunshine. If we keep petals tightly closed over the areas of life that are too painful to look at, He cannot come in. Open up to Christ the part in you that has been so hurt that you feel you can't ever trust human love again, you can't trust people. That feeling is understandable, but God is not asking you to trust people initially; He is asking you to trust Him, to trust Him with that part of you. You will find that Christ is different from other people: His love is different from human love. If you just allow Him, He will heal totally. I have absolutely no doubt about that. No matter how deep or longstanding the hurt, I have absolutely no doubt that Christ can heal in a moment the unbearable part, if you will let Him. If you will just give Him an opening for the chink of light to come in, His love can heal to the very uttermost and bring you through into freedom where your being is wide open to the sunshine of God and His love. Amen.

Diana

It is very interesting to hear what Grace has to say, because I also found the conflict before the camp extremely severe. I don't think I have ever known it to be more so on any previous occasion. It went on for quite a number of weeks.

To sketch the background of the earlier July camp, I had not managed out to as many meetings as I would have liked, largely because of the children, and felt very much that I was in the place of prayer and of carrying part of the burden for the work. I was very aware of the assault that there was in spiritual places and was burdened to fight through against that assault. By the end it really was glorious. After most of a week of conflict, something critical happened on the very last night. I was ministering to someone, still not knowing where the seat of the conflict lay or why it was quite so sustained and bitter. Normally the reason would become evident much earlier. But as I ministered that night, I saw that Satan was trying to prevent a particular life coming under phenomenal anointing against his own kingdom, and as this life came closer I saw such a hatred in Satan against that level of anointing, and I saw the tremendous victory of Christ. Christ Himself totally defeated the powers of darkness in that one moment of time. Then I understood the sense of fighting and being in the place of prayer for that week. It is glorious how a battle (and I'm not speaking about the battle for the whole camp; I'm speaking about the battle I was involved in) can be changed in a moment of time. One minute the tides of darkness were still coming in, and in a split second the position changed. God had come in and the powers of darkness had to flee.

The conflict during that July week had been so intense that the person with whom I was sharing my caravan said at the end of the week, 'I never want to share a caravan with you and your cronies* again!' — because she also had become aware from time to time of the darkness that came. Graham** and myself were sharing a caravan with different people in the August camp, and when I passed this information on beforehand they more or less exclaimed, 'Oh, no!'

Between the July and August camps I found quite a horrific sense of conflict. It reached the worst point on the Thursday night before the second occasion. I have never known such vile, intense conflict as I knew on that night. I was actually surprised at my reaction, because the battle became so intense that part of me almost gave in. I said, 'I'm not fighting any more. I don't want to have any further part in this battle. I'm just not going on.' Then I stopped and was shocked at my own reaction. I had never done such a thing before. I tend to be the kind of person that will fight to the very last breath. I left the Thursday night prayer meeting and went home angry with myself, and angry with the devil. I got home and I told him he would never do that

---

* Meaning the assaulting powers of darkness.
** Diana's husband.

to me again. I realized that he might well bring that level of assault against my life again, but I would never again give in. And on the Saturday night before the August camp began, I found that God brought me right through, the darkness completely lifted, and I went right out into the phenomenal glory of God. I was caught up, and looked round to see where that darkness had gone. It had completely gone; there was just no sense of it left.

ANTICIPATION OF VICTORY: So I went to camp with a tremendous sense of anticipation that there would be wonderful victory. If there had been such conflict, then God surely would come in and move in real power. I was aware of the need for Mr Black's sermon on deliverance. From time to time this kind of knowledge comes very clearly. I find this quite fascinating. Sometimes if I am present when Mr Black is ministering away from home and preaching on deliverance I find that the Holy Spirit begins to point out lives to me in the company and speaks to me about them, giving inner revelation of their condition and of their need for God. I nearly always find that these people come to me at the end, or are sent to me by Mr Black for ministry. I don't find it happens so much in our own home setting, because it is not so much needed (it does happen from time to time). But it did happen early in the camp, even before deliverance was preached. The Holy Spirit pointed out three lives to me, and the condition that they were in. Two of them came at the end of one meeting and were gloriously met by God, coming right through into a place of victory.

DELIVERANCE PREACHING AND MINISTRY: On the Wednesday morning Mr Black preached on deliverance, and between thirty and forty stayed behind at the end for ministry. Sometimes I find that ministry sessions can be quite difficult. But on this occasion I found that people were being met very easily and very wonderfully. They were also very hungry for God. Three cases particularly live for me. For one lady I felt very, very sorry. She had been through such horrific conflict in her life, knowing for two-and-a-half years of a need for deliverance, but being unable to find that place of freedom. She came desperately hungry for God, just waiting for Him to move. Within a matter of minutes, she was delivered and set free. It was lovely to see just how happy a person could be. I had seen the pain and hurt on her face. This thing had remained within her for so long, and Christ took it away in a moment of time.

For the second life there was quite a battle, but again the Holy Spirit came wonderfully, and there was glorious freedom. Sometimes people know they need deliverance. This man knew it and had known it for years. Again and again he had been ministered to in various parts of the country, and had responded to a level, but in his own words it was as though the demon in him got stuck and wouldn't come any further. He came to that point again — but, you know, it is the anointing that sets men free. It is not done in our strength or by our own power. He was encouraged to go right in under the anointing of God and was totally liberated. The change in his face and the change within him were obvious. He got up and walked away a bit overcome and bewildered by his experience. As he staggered off, he suddenly turned round and said, 'I feel wonderful! It's gone!' I love it when somebody is as clear as that.

The third was a lady whom Mr Black sent to me last night. Her condition was so awful that her circumstances could not be publicly revealed. She had carried pain for over twenty years: terrible, terrible pain. She had also recently known the death of a child. I felt deeply sorry for her. As she was speaking, the hurt showed visibly. She had been saved for a year, but had never been baptized in the Holy Spirit. We turned to prayer and she had a lovely baptism. There came a measure of healing in her life, and she went away much happier than she had come.

Kathleen

AN INNER WEEPING: Mr Black has asked me to share something that happened to me at camp, in relation to commitment.

I found before I went to camp that there had been a kind of grief inside me. At first I was a bit puzzled, and I thought, there's nobody I know who has died. It was like a sense of mourning, and I couldn't understand it at first. Then I began just to try to listen to what the Spirit inside me was saying, and a verse came to me: *Godly sorrow leads to repentance.* I felt as though there was a sorrow inside, and it was related to a lack of commitment and a lack of drive manifest in my life from time to time over the past few years.

A LACK OF COMMITMENT: At camp on the Wednesday night I had come before the Lord and had acknowledged the truth of this: I had been quite casual from time to time. It never ceased to amaze me how much God was prepared to bless me, or how He would pour out His love on me again and again. Sometimes I felt really ashamed when I thought of the kind of half-hearted response there was in me. It was not always like that, but there were times when I knew very clearly that it was. I was quite challenged when Bill Marks was speaking recently about something similar.[1]

I thought, 'I'm very much in that position as well. I've committed my life to God, but there's a great deal that I keep to myself, a lot of will that is unbroken.'

Over the past few Saturday nights there has been opportunity to respond to this call to deeper commitment, to resolve that one will no longer retain self-will, but will allow it to be broken up, and to be totally open to God coming in and filling every part of one's life. I wanted that to happen, but I found that I couldn't really respond to that invitation because of the seriousness of it. I never take these things lightly. I never make a response unless I feel that my spirit is ready. I find sometimes that one can get carried along on an emotional tide — and I'm not decrying that for a moment, because I'm quite an emotional person myself. But I felt that there was something that prevented me from truly committing myself at that level, and I did not want a merely emotional commitment. A great part of the problem was fear, I think: fear of what it would mean, fear of the change it would bring, and a reluctance to give over the parts of self that I had retained. But by the time I went to camp I had been aware of a kind of mourning, and it had been leading to a genuine repentance. I felt, 'God, I am truly sorry that I haven't responded to You as fully as I know I should have, and as fully as I know that You have wanted me to.'

That night, in my heart I genuinely wanted the real strength of God to come into the very deeps of me. I came back from that camp meeting feeling more determined: I really did want that iron strength of God. When I got up the next morning my heart sank, because physically I did not feel at all well. I felt very weak, not only spiritually, but physically also. When I got to the

camp again, I was intensely aware of how weak I felt
and what a weak person I was. I had asked God to break
up the resistance that was in me, and at the tarry meeting in the afternoon I found that He began to do it. It
was very painful in a way that brought tears, which I
tried to conceal, because I think there's a lot of pride in
me as well. Sometimes one likes to keep one's feelings
and intentions to oneself.

The thought came: 'Why are you surprised at feeling
so weak? — because you have prayed for My strength.'

That was the area that I felt the devil was really
assaulting. He was, I suppose, trying to make me focus
on just how weak I was. And I had a sense of a great big
rock in the middle of an awful lot of water. The water
seemed to represent my feeling of weakness and
instability. The rock in the midst of the water was like
the self-will. I was surprised at how large and solid it
was. I asked God to break it up, and was again aware of
His doing so. Returning home, I found it very difficult
to stop crying. I could hardly speak to anyone, because
whenever anyone addressed me I felt I wanted to cry.

MET BY GOD: On the Thursday night I was greatly
affected by the preaching, particularly the first verse
that was quoted: *Because thine heart was tender, and
thou didst humble thyself before the LORD...I also have
heard thee, saith the LORD* (2 Ki 22:19). That really
spoke to me. As we moved into a time of worship later,
so much had been accomplished even before I came to
the camp that the way was opened for a new experience.

It was as if there was a rainbow coming towards me,
and as it came nearer and nearer, it seemed to break up.
As this happened, the reds and yellows receded, and
the deepest of the colours seemed to be descending

round about me. They were recognizable as blues and purples, yet in shades I had not seen before. It seemed possible to touch their velvet substance. The atmosphere was charged with their splendour; as I was journeying through colours of such depth and glory it was as though they were actually heralding the presence of the Lord Jesus Himself.

And yet when I went home that night I still found it so difficult to make that decision. It was as though there was something inside that just would not let go. From the moment of waking on the Friday morning I had a feeling of dread and of struggle. Suddenly I remembered what it had been like just before I was converted. I had had an awful struggle before I became a Christian. It lasted for weeks. I was hardly able to sleep because of the depth of the struggle that went on. Now it was the same kind of feeling again, the same kind of dread in the pit of my stomach, the same awful difficulty. I thought, 'I'm never going to be able to make this depth of commitment. I just don't seem to have it in me.'

Then it was as though God said to me, 'What would your life have been like these past twenty years had you not made that first commitment? If you had not overcome that opposition and that feeling and that grip that was within you, what would your life have been?'

In a flash I was filled with gratitude for what my life has been over those years. It has certainly been very far from perfect, but God has been so gracious; He has been so wonderful. I thought not only of what God had done in my own life, but what He had done in the lives of my family as well. What I felt He was saying to me was, 'If you have known that blessing through making that first commitment, what is awaiting you if you are prepared to make this one?' I suddenly wanted to do it. For the first time there was a genuine desire to do so.

VICTORY: When I went back to camp on the Friday morning, I wondered whether I should actually go for ministry. I was very open to doing so, if it was right for me. The invitation came, as it had done at the end of most of the meetings, to respond if we were willing to go all the way with God, to give over the control and the decision-making rights that we like to retain. Outwardly I was probably very calm; inwardly my heart was really pounding, and I had almost to force myself to do it. But the moment I raised my hand as a sign of my decision, the struggle totally ceased, and I found a tremendous sense of peace and well-being and strength in God. I was thrilled that God had been prepared to wait as long as He did to have this deeper commitment. I know that there may be other critical choices ahead. But I feel that I have made the degree of commitment called for at this present time. What rejoices my heart is that God keeps that which we commit unto Him. Paul could say, *I am persuaded that he is able to keep that which I have committed unto him against that day* (2 Tim 1:12). God knows how weak I am, He knows what I am like, and yet because I have been real with Him, I know that He has taken me and I know that He will keep for me too that which I have committed to Him.

PRAYER: *Lord our God, there is a joy in our hearts at the triumph of Christ, the overcoming by the Lamb of God in the lives of men, the heel of the seed of the woman on the head of the serpent, and the victory that is and for ever shall be. Lord, we declare the triumph of Christ. We pray that Your people will look upward and rejoice in the Lord, as Paul could say, Rejoice...and again I say unto thee, Rejoice. And we would joy in the God of our salvation. Be with us now, we ask, in the name Lord Jesus Christ and for His sake. Amen.*

Note

1 This is one of our fellowship who in vision or dream was addressed after his death by Christ in sadness and was told how he could have done so much more for Him if he had been fully committed. His life was profoundly affected by this experience.

9 | A CLUSTER OF HEALINGS

The following healings are appropriately described as a 'cluster', since three of them were linked together and all of them happened within a short space of time in the summer of 1992 to members of our branch church in Port Glasgow. The following account was given verbally by Joan Jewell, the leader in charge. It is interspersed with additional information culled from the individuals concerned, the last of whom also had her testimony recorded on tape.

Janice

On quite a few occasions lately God has given instant healing. The first case was Janice.

One night her friend Agnes, who had recently been saved and baptized in the Spirit, said, without going into detail, that Janice was not very well. I arranged to see her after our Friday night meeting. Agnes had let her know I was coming and was with her when I arrived. Janice answered the door in her dressing-gown and was obviously unwell. There seemed something wrong with her neck, for her head was held to one side, and her arm was twisted. We chatted for a minute or two. Agnes and I were sitting on one settee, and Janice was on the other side of the room. I went over and prayed with her and then sat down. And this, I think, is the really lovely part. Jesus just came walking into the room. It was as though He opened the door and walked in, just like that. There came such a freedom and a light. Although He was invisible, it was like talking with a person who was really there.

I opened my eyes and looked across at Janice. I saw her opening her eyes and moving her head freely. Of course I was overjoyed, and nudged Agnes to look as well. Janice then lifted her arm up as high as she could and put it down again. I didn't say anything to her afterwards, nor did she to me, although I was longing to know what had happened. On the following night, she told me that on the Friday morning a muscle spasm had given her an excruciating pain in her back — the worst she had ever had. She went to the doctor and was prescribed three different types of pills. After the Friday night healing she regained movement in her arm, and then her neck and her head. She was left with a tiny bit of pain still at the back of her neck, but that soon disappeared. And so God gets the glory.

FURTHER DETAIL: It had turned out that Janice was allergic to one of the drugs. In her own words she had been 'as high as a kite', but by the time Joan arrived was feeling groggy with the effects of the medication. The grogginess disappeared as soon as she was prayed with. The reality of Janice's healing was plain to see when she went cycling for ten miles round the island of Millport on the following day.

Agnes and Kirsty

The next Friday night Agnes's husband Danny was at the meeting.

'And where's Agnes?' I asked.

'Oh, she's hurt her back and she's in bed.'

I thought, 'This is getting to be a regular thing!' To Danny I said, 'I'll come up and see her after the meeting.'

I took Janice with me and we went up to their top flat. Agnes was confined to her attic bedroom. Her little daughter Kirsty was in bed beside her mother, for she too wasn't well. Daniel was sitting on the ottoman, and mother and daughter were lying flat out on the bed. We chatted and then we prayed. I went over to pray with Kirsty that God would touch her, because she had a temperature; I didn't realize then that she had been vomiting the day before and was really sick. She was due to go on holiday with a friend's parents the next morning. I had intended to pray simply that Jesus would make her better, and found myself praying with her for the baptism in the Spirit. There came again that lovely freedom. It was as though Christ walked into the room, and you just lost sight of everybody else. It was like being in another dimension, not on earth, but in a spiritual dimension where Christ was. All of us felt it. Kirsty came beautifully into her baptism.

Then I went to Agnes and asked God to touch her as well. God was moving: there was such a freedom you couldn't stop praying. We all went into worship and forgot about each other. I opened my eyes — which I'm not usually in the habit of doing — and looked at Kirsty. There she was lying flat out on her bed beside her mum, with her two hands up, speaking in tongues, oblivious of everybody! I nudged Janice to look at Kirsty, so that she could share in the joy as well.

As with Janice earlier, I didn't know what had happened to Agnes. When she came out to the Saturday night meeting, I thought perhaps she was a bit better. But she didn't say anything to me. On the Sunday morning I asked her to come and tell the company what had happened to Kirsty on the Friday (Kirsty was away on holiday by this time). I didn't ask Agnes to testify to healing, because at that point I didn't know if anything had happened. But the first thing she said was that God had healed her.

She had been in the kitchen on the Thursday morning, bending down, and couldn't straighten up. Something had gone wrong with a lower disc. Since she was too unwell to go to the doctor, Janice contacted him for her. He came and told her to lie on a board for about ten days, and to use ointment and take painkillers and sleeping pills. During that period of time she was not to go out at all. She could not even come downstairs to see us in the lounge when we arrived. But just after we went away she got up and went to the bathroom, and there was no pain, no need for tablets; nothing at all. God had touched her in healing.

And of course when Kirsty came back from her holiday, she was asked to tell what had happened to her — because I don't think it's fair that somebody else should give your testimony for you! So she told how she was baptized in the Holy Spirit and healed. Her temperature went down, the vomiting stopped, and she was well enough to go on her holiday the next day. The whole episode was really lovely.

FURTHER DETAIL: Agnes confirmed that she had been prescribed such strong painkillers and sleeping pills that the chemist insisted on verifying the prescription by a telephone call to the Health Centre — to Janice's embarrassment. Yet at the moment Joan prayed with her she was so caught up in God that she was not even aware that her body was being healed — though she realized it immediately afterwards.

Kirsty had suffered through her childhood from two serious conditions. One was a bad kidney which made her prone to the kind of viral infection and high temperatures that she had on the night of her healing. She had spent much of her time between Yorkhill Hospital for Sick Children and Inverclyde Royal Hospital, and an operation was in prospect. Frequent hospitalization and poor attendance at school were her routine experience. The other problem was a blood disease (*Idiopathic thrombocytopoenic purpura*) characterized by internal bleeding which caused bruising all over her body.

Never once since her healing has Kirsty been hospitalized, though she has continued to have regular check-ups, in case any further deterioration of the kidney should necessitate an operation. The doctor who examined her during her last visit to Yorkhill Hospital (about five weeks before this book was due to go to print) could scarcely believe that it was the same girl. He gave her a clean bill of health. Before her healing she had been on an adult course of tablets daily; she has since been taken completely off her medication.

In the session following her healing Kirsty gained weight, achieved excellent attendance at school, and was runner-up to the Sports Champion of the year!

Isabel

Isabel had been in hospital before the July camp, and still wasn't too well. She had had a pain in her side before she went to hospital, and was also on antibiotics for an ear infection. While she was at camp she was obviously unwell. The pain that had taken her to hospital was back worse than ever. Wakening at four o'clock one morning she had thought of coming for me, but felt she couldn't disturb me so early — even though I was only a few feet away in the caravan next door. The next day she asked me to come and see her. I suggested, 'Why don't we go and get Mr Black to pray for you?' She said, 'No, you pray for me.'*

So we prayed. And again there came that same sense that 'Christ is here, and anything could happen.' It filled the caravan. There was that freedom, and the presence of Christ. He was just there. When I left her I did not know what had happened, but she came the next day looking much brighter and told me that the pain had gone from her side.

FURTHER DETAIL: It was in connection with the pain in her side that Isabel had been admitted to hospital for tests. These were inconclusive. The pain that woke her in the middle of the night in her caravan was so severe (far beyond anything she has known before or since) that she thought she would have to go home. But when Joan prayed with her and there came the intense awareness of Christ, the pain left her and has never returned. Whether for the same reason or for more mundane causes, the ear infection has caused no further trouble.

Doreen

Last Sunday morning Doreen came to me just before the service started and said, 'Joan, I'm not feeling well at all. I don't want to go into the details, because we're just about to start the service. But please remember me.'

There was no preaching that Sunday morning. During

---

* At this point in Joan's narrative, there was heard a loud *Amen* from Mr Black.

the time of prayer I felt directed to go over to her; I prayed very briefly and left her. This is the thing I think is absolutely lovely: you leave them, and Christ just comes along, and He touches them! I think she should maybe tell you herself what happened. God healed her and He made her feel a hundred per cent better. She phoned me the next morning, and she said, 'I must tell you what happened in the service.'

Christ came into the service, and Christ ministered to her, Christ Himself: the Person of the Lord Jesus Christ came and ministered to her. It was altogether lovely.

So you can see how encouraged we all are that God is moving in our midst, and I hope that encourages all of you as well.

DOREEN SPEAKS FOR HERSELF: It was last week that I had become quite unwell and trotted off to the doctor, who prescribed antibiotics. A few days elapsed and the pills (give them their due) did take effect. But apart from that I did not feel well at all, and I just couldn't put my finger on what was wrong. I kept saying to myself, 'I'll give it another day and I'll feel a bit better.' But I didn't, and the trouble persisted. If it hadn't been for my two children I would have quite happily gone into bed, pulled up the covers, and that would have been that. On the Sunday morning I was really tempted to stay at home because I felt so ill, but one half of me wanted to go, knowing I would miss out if I didn't go. As Joan said, I asked when I went in if I could have prayer.

When Joan prayed with me I was very conscious of something that came to my mind. It was the picture of a door, a square door, as if away at the end of a long passageway. And it was as if the Lord was saying to me, 'You've to aim for that door. Go through.' It reminded me of the veil in the temple that was rent in two. Whereas the priest could only go in once a year, now there is free access. And that was where He wanted me to aim. Then as the morning meeting progressed, all of a sudden during the worship I was aware that there was somebody beside me. I knew it wasn't a physical presence, but it was as real as a physical presence. Words could not describe it. It was fantastic, absolutely fantastic.

I felt as if there was something on top of my head; something warm, slowly, very, very slowly coming down over my head. And this is the ironical thing about it: what He did heal was a complaint I have had for years, something I lived with — it didn't really bother me very much at all! I've always had problems with my neck; you just live with it and forget about it. But as this was happening I became conscious of my neck. It was as if all the little bones in my neck were suddenly in a knot, and then I felt as if my whole being was totally enclosed in something I could not identify. I could not have moved out of that seat for anything. If a bomb had gone off, I would still have been sitting there; I could not have moved. It was absolutely wonderful! Then I suddenly thought, 'Here, I do feel better! This is good, I really do feel better.'

Shortly after that the meeting finished. It was the next morning that it came home to me what had happened, because always in the morning when I got up I would have a terribly stiff neck, though as a rule it would gradually wear off as I moved around. But I woke up that morning with absolutely no stiffness in my neck at all. And every morning this week I've had no pain, no stiffness, nothing. It has been fantastic. But all week, as it has been in my mind, what has been so wonderful is the joy and the thrill of realizing what

Christ has done for me. It has filled me up to overflow-
ing.

Mr Black's Comments

There is something very lovely in Joan's speaking
tonight and in what we have heard from Doreen. We
became conscious not of a wonderful person with a
wonderful gift; that's often a human way of looking at
these things. We became conscious of a wonderful
Christ who walked with men, who came into these
rooms and into these occasions. He filled with the Holy
Spirit, He healed bodies, and He revealed Himself. And
I want you to open your spirit for the revelation of the
Lord Jesus Christ moving from seat to seat, from heart
to heart.

For readers, a word of encouragement: many, many
have been healed since these incidents less than a year
ago.

> He healeth yet,
> Though the sun be set
> On the Galilean hills.

Come and have faith in God.

Conclusion

These healings are an indication of the kind of phe-
nomenon that is likely to become more prominent with
the coming of revival. The reader cannot fail to have
noticed how Christ-centred they were, both in the manner of their occurrence and in the telling of them.

Throughout this book we have seen something of
what is involved in revival living — living in the realities: deepening sanctification, new planes of holiness,

a maturing in Christ, Christ becoming more manifestly alive in us, an expectation of deepening works of power, and miracles (including healings), as the order of the day. We must prepare for what is expected of us with perfect confidence in the part God will play.

Let hope shine like a star and lead to anticipation and on to faith — a faith not to be denied. May I wish all my readers the blessing of God.

NOTE TO READERS

If you would like to enquire further about issues raised in this book or if you feel that the author could be of help, you are invited to write to him at 27 Denholm Street, Greenock, PA16 8RH, Scotland, or telephone 0475 87432.

It may also be of interest to know that the author is normally involved in five conferences in Scotland each year — New Year, Easter, July, August and October. Friends gather from many parts of Britain. An open invitation is extended to all and particularly to those interested in the Baptism in the Holy Spirit and related themes. Details will be provided on enquiry.

BY THE SAME AUTHOR

Reflections on the Baptism in the Holy Spirit *£2.25*
This book is already proving very popular and is being
used in bringing people into the baptism in the Spirit.
It has been described as one of the clearest, most inci-
sive books on this subject.

Reflections on the Gifts of the Spirit *£2.75* Deals in an
original way with its subject. The chapters on miracles,
healings and discernment (with exorcism) have roused
great interest and led to positive action. Anecdotes and
illustrations have been much appreciated.

Reflections on a Song of Love *£1.25* A highly original
commentary on 1 Cor 13. The drawing power of love
pervades this fascinating study. The author shows very
clearly how this chapter fully supports and in no way
detracts from the doctrine of Pentecost.

A Trumpet Call to Women *£2.50* Presents a strong case
from Scripture for greater involvement of women in
ministry. It throws much light on those portions which
on the surface seem to put women in a subject role. It
includes the testimony of Elizabeth H. Taylor, a lady
much used of God. A stirring book, demanding a
response — a call to action.

Consider Him *£2.25* Considers a number of the
qualities of Christ. He Himself seems to speak from the

pages of the book, both in the main text and in the testimony of Jennifer Jack, whose selfless presentation truly leaves the reader to consider Christ.

Battle for the Body £2.95 It will take courage to face the truths highlighted in this original approach to fundamental issues of sanctification. The second part presents the powerful testimony of John Hamilton — a preacher widely known and loved.

The Clash of Tongues: With Glimpses of Revival £2.75 Part One is a commentary on 1 Cor 14. It deals in detail with some of the more difficult questions. Part Two deals with the relationship between revival and Pentecost and refers to the 1939 and 1949 revivals in Lewis, introducing a number of people who were involved in the first of these — particularly Mary MacLean, whose remarkable testimony is related. This book may particularly appeal to people studiously inclined.

The Incomparable Christ £2.75 Part One deals with the gospel. It faces honestly the questions of Christ's resurrection and that of all men. It deals in a direct way with the doctrine of hell and eternal judgment, and gives practical instruction on the way of salvation. Part Two presents the remarkable testimonies of two young ladies.

Gospel Vignettes £2.95 Focuses attention on various facets of the gospel, with chapter titles like: Ye Must Be Born Again, The Life-Giving Water, Weighed in the Balances, Behold I Stand at the Door and Knock, The Hour of Decision. Includes testimonies of three people whose lives have been transformed by Christ, to one of whom Christ Himself appeared. Useful in the gospel, but introducing the Pentecostal dimension.

Reflections from Abraham *£2.50* Outlines spiritual principles seen in the life of Abraham. It deals with his call and ours, the mountain as distinct from the valley life, intercession, Lot in Sodom, the sacrifice of Isaac and the way of faith. Part Two tells of the action of God in the life of Dorothy Jennings, to whom Abraham has been of particular significance.

Reflections from Moses: With the Testimony of Dan McVicar *£2.99* Part One shows the outworking of spiritual principles such as the calling and training of a man of God, the need to start from holy ground, deliverance from bondage, and the consequences of Moses' failure in a critical hour. Part Two presents the well-known evangelist Dan McVicar's story in his own words. The conversion of this militant communist and the intervention of God in the lives of his parents make thrilling reading.

Christ the Deliverer *£2.99* Deals with both physical and spiritual deliverance. It includes a number of remarkable testimonies to healing, e.g. from blindness, manic depression, ME, rheumatoid arthritis, spinal injury, phobias, nightmares. It speaks of the appearance of angels, touches on revival and analyses the theory of 'visualization'.

Christian Fundamentals *£3.50* Part One deals with the individual and his needs in the realms of Salvation, Baptism in the Spirit, and Deliverance. Part Two focuses on the outflow of the life of God to meet the needs of others through Vocal, Hidden and Open Power Ministries. The End Times are the subject of Part Three.

Reflections from David £3.75 This searching book shows a man after God's own heart in the glory of his achievements and the tragedy of his failings. Divine retribution and forgiveness, the joy of deliverance, and the action of God in present-day lives are all examined.

Pioneers of the Spiritual Way £4.99 From a lost Eden our race walked a lost road, occasionally experiencing higher things as pioneers of the spiritual way led upwards. The impassable barrier between God and man was finally removed as the last Adam blasted a way through: Christ, bringing many sons to glory.

Revival: Including the Prophetic Vision of Jean Darnall £3.99 Some of the great revivals of the past are reviewed with their enduring principles and changing patterns. Revival comes nearer as we are confronted with more recent movements of God. The celebrated vision of Jean Darnall has left many with a feeling of keen expectation for coming days.

Revival: Personal Encounters £4.50 From the treasure chest of memory the author brings a series of revival-related incidents. We hear of Studd, Burton and Salter and of revival in the Congo and Rwanda. More is revealed of the moving of God in Lewis and at an unusual Scottish school camp. A contemporary scene in Brazil brings revival very close. The highly original testimony of Alison Speirs brings the fact and challenge right to our doorstep.

BOOK ORDERS

The books advertised on the previous pages are being made available to Christian booksellers throughout the country, but if you have any difficulty in obtaining your supply, you may order directly from New Dawn Books, c/o 27 Denholm Street, Greenock, Scotland, PA16 8RH.

· · · · · · · · · · · · · · ORDER FORM · · · · · · · · · · · · · ·

Please send me the books indicated below:

Quantity	Title	Price
	Reflections on the Baptism in the Holy Spirit	£2.25
	Reflections on the Gifts of the Spirit	£2.75
	Reflections on a Song of Love (A commentary on 1 Cor 13)	£1.25
	A Trumpet Call to Women	£2.50
	Consider Him (Twelve Qualities of Christ)	£2.25
	Battle for the Body	£2.95
	The Clash of Tongues: With Glimpses of Revival	£2.75
	The Incomparable Christ	£2.75
	Gospel Vignettes	£2.95
	Reflections from Abraham	£2.50
	Reflections from Moses: With the Testimony of Dan McVicar	£2.99
	Christ the Deliverer	£2.99
	Christian Fundamentals	£3.50
	Reflections from David	£3.75
	Pioneers of the Spiritual Way	£4.99
	Revival: Including the Prophetic Vision of Jean Darnall	£3.99
	Revival: Personal Encounters	£4.50
	Revival: Living in the Realities	£3.99

Signature . . . .

Address . . . .

. . . .

. . . .

When ordering please send purchase price plus 40p per book to help cover the cost of postage and packaging.